THE HISTORY OF
FLY-FISHING
IN FIFTY FLIES

DEDICATION

Ian and Julie wish to dedicate this book to their father, Robert Whitelaw, "with fond memories of the many happy hours we spent together on the riverbank when I was a boy," and "with thanks for all the support and encouragement that you have given me over the years."

Published in 2015 by Abrams Image

Library of Congress Control Number: 2014942977

ISBN: 978-1-61769-146-1

Printed and bound in China

11

Abrams Image books are available at special discounts when purchased in quantity for premiums and promotions as well as fundraising or educational use. Special editions can also be created to specification. For details, contact specialsales@abramsbooks.com or the address below.

ABRAMS The Art of Books
195 Broadway, New York, NY 10007
abramsbooks.com

MIX
Paper from
responsible sources
FSC
www.fsc.org   FSC® C017606

THE HISTORY OF

FLY-FISHING

IN FIFTY FLIES

IAN WHITELAW

Illustrations by Julie Spyropoulos

CONTENTS

Introduction

Fishing has often been referred to as an art as much as a sport,
and in the case of fly fishing the artistry extends beyond the practice
to the creation of the flies themselves. Carefully designed and tied,
often delicate and intricate, the flies are a large part of what makes
fly fishing so enjoyable, so what better way to examine the history
of the sport than through a chronological sequence of fifty flies?

NO WEIGHT, NO BAIT

Three of the many plates from Mary Orvis Marbury's Favorite Flies and Their Histories *show the colour and variety in North American wet flies towards the end of the 19th century. The dry fly was about to change the picture radically.*

You might ask 'Which fifty flies?', but let's start with a more basic question. What is a fly? The term 'artificial fly' was already being used in the 16th century to include caterpillars and worms, and over the intervening years it has been applied to larvae, nymphs, leeches, baitfish, frogs and, in the case of carp flies, even berries and seeds, so it clearly doesn't just mean a representation of a flying insect. Our definition is something that is too light to be cast any distance without a fly line, has no food-like scent or taste and is designed to fool a fish into eating it only by its appearance and behaviour.

A fly tyer's desk in the mid 1940s reveals traditional materials such as pheasant tail feathers, rooster capes and silk tying thread. Within a few decades these would be joined by a host of synthetic materials, opening new avenues for the tyer.

HOOKS TO HANG THE HISTORY ON

That narrows it down to just a few thousand patterns, so how have the fifty been chosen? There is no one answer, because they have been chosen for a variety of reasons. Some are milestones in the history of fly tying, some are here as representatives of broad classes of fly, some act as a focal point around which to discuss broader issues within the sport, some are examples of the possibilities opened up by the discovery or invention of particular fly-tying materials, and some allow us to explore the larger-than-life characters who created them. Some are just too effective to leave out. Each of them has a story that extends far beyond itself to include the flies that led up to it and those that it inspired or that embody similar principles or materials. Together they chart the evolution of fly fishing, the increasing diversity and sophistication of flies, the widening range of fish species that are being caught on the fly, and the geographical spread of the sport.

Above all they chart our deepening understanding of the natural world – of the fish themselves, their behaviour and perception, the items on which they feed, their habitats and the ecosystems of which they are a part. This, after all, is the knowledge

'It is not every man who should go a-fishing, but there are many who would find this their true rest and recreation of body and mind. And having…learned by experience how pleasant it is to go a-fishing, you will find…that you are drawn to it whenever you are weary, impatient, or sad.'
W.C. Prime, Go A-Fishing

Its buoyancy and versatility have made deer hair a staple in the dry fly tyer's toolkit since the 19th century. As well as forming many different kinds of wing, it can be spun and sculpted to create shaped bodies and heads.

on which the art and science of fly fishing are founded and we need as much knowledge as possible, for, as John Steinbeck once wrote, 'It has always been my private conviction that any man who pits his intelligence against a fish and loses has it coming.'

FIFTY AND THE REST

Eyed hooks started to become popular in the later part of the 19th century, but eyeless hooks whipped to gut remained in use well into the 20th.

For each fly we list the year in which it was first tied, by whom and where, and a watercolour illustration depicts the fly in its original form. Schematic diagrams show what materials are – or were – used to make each part of the fly. Each of the fifty flies is really a starting point, and as the story of each one unfolds, connections with other flies and other fly tyers are made, and trends in the practice of fly fishing appear. The materials used change from basic, locally available fur and feathers to the most exotic and colourful plumage from around the world, then to dyed replacements for endangered feathers and finally to a host of synthetic materials and new breeds of fly.

Changes in the technology of fishing both affect and are affected by the evolution of fly design, and interspersed throughout

the book there are 'State of the Art' sections that summarise the development of rods, reels, lines and hooks in each of the last three centuries.

Finally, there is a bibliography of fly fishing books and a list of useful websites, as well as a mention of some of the many anglers, fly tyers and historians who have so generously helped to put this book together.

WHEN DOES THE HISTORY START?

No discussion of the origins of fly fishing can fail to mention the first known description of the use of an artifical fly. Claudius Aelianus (or Aelian), the Roman author of *On the Nature of Animals*, writing in about 200 CE, tells us that in Macedonia (now northern Greece) there is a small fly called Hippouros that looks a bit like a wasp, hums like a bee and is eaten by fish when it lands on the water. Fishermen don't use the fly as bait because 'if a man's hand touch them, they lose their natural colour, their wings wither, and they become unfit food for the fish.' Instead, the local anglers wrap a hook with crimson red wool and attach two wax coloured feathers from a cockerel's throat (presumably as wings). Using 6ft (1.8m) of line on a 6ft (1.8m) rod, they cast this out and the fish go for it and get hooked. It isn't clear why the artificial fly is red while the natural looks like a wasp, but this is undoubtedly fly fishing. It has come a long way since then.

'No angler merely watches nature in a passive way. He enters into its very existence.' **John Bailey,** ***Reflections from the Water's Edge***

Early morning on a placid lake, a few rises dimpling the surface and no commitments for the rest of the day — what could be better?

Stonefly

YEAR: 1496   **FLY TYER:** Dame Juliana Berners   **LOCATION:** Hertfordshire, England

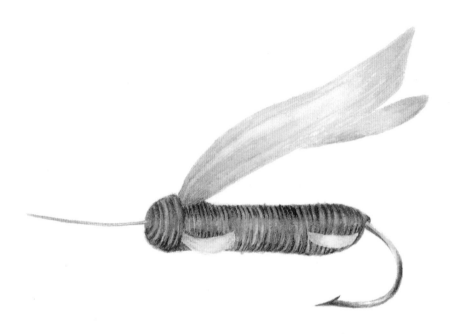

The **Original Recipe**

Hook
Handmade from a bent and tempered needle, with a hand-cut barb

Body
Black wool

Thorax / Abdomen
Yellow wool under the wing and under the tail

Head
Black wool

Wings
Drake feather slips

Tippet
Horse hair whipped to the hook

After brief references to fishing with what we would now call an artificial fly, almost nothing more was written on the subject for the next thousand years. Then, out of the blue, a book was printed in which the fully formed art of fishing with a hook was expounded in extraordinary detail. This very first angling literature included a list of twelve flies and the materials needed to tie them, and we've chosen the stonefly from that list as an example.

THE FISHING NUN?

The first edition of the *Boke of St Albans* (so called because it has no title page but was printed in the English town of St Albans) appeared in 1486 and comprised three essays on hawking, hunting and heraldry. A second edition, published in London ten years later by the renowned printer Wynkyn de Worde, successor to William Caxton, included a fourth essay entitled *Treatyse of Fisshynge wyth an Angle*. Although scholarly doubts about their authorship remain, the essays have been attributed to Dame Juliana Berners of the Order of Saint Benedict, Prioress of the Priory of St Mary of Sopwell, the ruins of which still stand on the east bank of the River Ver, just outside St Albans. The *Treatyse*, which was soon published separately from the other essays, proved to be a best seller and remained in print for the next hundred years.

It is clear from the writing that the author of the *Treatyse* is compiling a compendium of the accepted wisdom of the time and is drawing on earlier European treatises (of which little trace remains), rather than expressing her personal knowledge or opinions. Introducing the list of flies, for example, she says, 'These are the twelve flies with which you shall angle to the trout and grayling and dub them like you shall now hear me tell,' implying that the twelve are the patterns in use at the time and there are no others.

A 15th-century angler adds another fish to his basket. There is clearly a float on the line, but it would be several hundred years before a distinction was made between a float rod and a fly rod.

'*Also, you must not use this aforesaid artful sport for covetousness to increasing or saving of your money only, but principally for your solace and to promote the health of your body and specially of your soul.'* **Dame Juliana Berners**

The Twelve Flies According to Dame Juliana

The list, rewritten in more modern English, reads as follows:

March

1 The dun fly: the body of dun wool and the wings of the partridge.

2 Another dun fly: the body of black wool, the wings of the blackest drake, and the jay under the wing and under the tail.

April

3 The stonefly: the body of black wool, and yellow under the wing and under the tail, and the wings of the drake.

May

4 In the beginning of May, a good fly: the body of reddened wool and lapped about with black silk, the wings of the drake and the red capon's hackle.

5 The yellow fly: the body of yellow wool, the wings of red cock hackle and of the drake dyed yellow.

6 The black leaper: the body of black wool and lapped about with the herl of the peacock's tail and the wings of the red capon with a blue head.

June

7 The dun cut: the body of black wool, and a yellow stripe after either side, the wings of the buzzard, bound on with barked hemp.

8 The maure fly: the body of dusky wool, the wings of the blackest male of the wild drake.

9 The tandy fly at St William's Day: the body of tandy wool, and the wings contrary either against the other, of the whitest breast feathers of the wild drake.

July

10 The wasp fly: the body of black wool and lapped about with yellow thread, the wings of the buzzard.

11 The shell fly at St Thomas's Day: the body of green wool and lapped about with the herl of the peacock's tail, wings of the buzzard.

August

12 The drake fly: the body of black wool and lapped about with black silk, wings of the breast feathers of the blackest drake, with a black head.

These same twelve winged flies reappear almost unaltered in Leonard Mascall's *A Book of Fishing with Hooke and Line*, published in 1590, and again in Isaak Walton's *The Compleat Angler* (1653), in which he comments, 'Thus have you a jury of flies likely to betray and condemn all the Trouts in the river'.

What is so remarkable about this list, written more than 500 years ago, is that apart from words such as maure (ant) and tandy (tawny) it makes sense to any modern fly tyer. There is little in the way of tying instructions but the yarn, feathers, silk, thread and even the peacock herl are all there, and several illustrators and tyers have made very plausible attempts at replicating the original flies.

There has been considerable debate about which insects or modern fly patterns they represent or equate to but the consensus seems to be:

1 | February red or march brown
2 | Olive dun
3 | Stonefly
4 | Red spinner or great red spinner
5 | Little yellow may dun
6 | Sedge fly / caddis
7 | Yellow dun or sedge fly / caddis
8 | Green drake or alder fly
9 | Gray drake or oak fly
10 | Wasp
11 | Grannom or sedge fly / caddis
12 | Alder fly

In Dame Juliana's day the systematic study of insects was barely in its infancy, but the artificial flies were clearly designed to represent the naturals, such as this broad-headed stonefly illustrated in the classic British Entomology *by* John Curtis, *published in the 19th century.*

WET OR DRY?

Looking at the modern version of the list, today's fly fisher's first thought is likely to be 'dry flies' but none of these flies is likely to have floated for long before becoming waterlogged and sinking beneath the surface. The angler would have had to use the rod to keep the fly on or close to the surface. The dressings are suggestive of fully formed winged adults as they might appear at rest out of the water and although some of these species do emerge and become adults beneath the surface, these are not what we would now call emerger patterns. Nor are they likely to have looked like drowned adults, being relatively stiff winged rather than floppy and mobile in the current. Nonetheless, these and other winged wet patterns were to constitute the bulk of the fly angler's armoury for the next 350 years!

Admittedly, the adults of some caddis species do swim down through the water to lay their eggs, and the hard-winged alder fly does sink if it falls in the river, so some of the twelve could have looked like the naturals, but winged wet patterns were – and still can be – extremely effective.

THE STATE OF THE ART IN 1500

*A*s well as extolling the virtues of angling – and of the angler – Dame Juliana's essay deals in considerable detail with many practical aspects of 'fishing with a hook,' telling the reader when and where to fish, how to prepare baits of various kinds and which baits to use for each kind of fish. Most importantly, she describes the fishing tackle of the time and explains how to make it, giving us a fascinating insight into the angling technology of the time.

The Rod

'And howe you shall make your rod craftely, here I shall teache you, ye shall cut betweene Michelmas & Candelmas a fayre staffe of a fadome and a halfe longe and arme great of hasyll, wyllowe or aspe…'

Or, to put it another way, start by cutting for yourself – between the dates of 29 September and 2 February – a 9ft (2.7m) staff of hazel, willow or ash as thick as your arm. This staff must be placed in a hot oven and straightened before being allowed to dry for a month. Now bind it to a large and perfectly flat piece of wood and, using successively thicker red-hot metal rods, bore a tapering hole through the staff before placing it in the smoky roof space of your house to dry it thoroughly.

In the meantime, cut a 3ft (90cm) green hazel stick, soak it and straighten it and place it to dry with the staff. When they are both dry, make sure the hazel stick fits all the way into the staff. It will form half of the top section of your rod. The tip half is made from blackthorn, crabtree, medlar or juniper wood. Bind this to the end of the hazel and the two together should fit inside the bottom section. Now shave your staff down to give it a taper, bind it with a metal ring top and bottom (presumably to prevent it from splitting), and fix a metal catch at the bottom to hold the top section inside. Whittle the bottom end of the top section so that it fits inside the top of the bottom section, tie on a loop of horsehair at the tip (to which your fishing line will be attached), and you're ready to go. This rod, we are told, 'wyll be very lyght & nymble to fyshe with at your pleasure….' What's more, as you walk along with your smooth and tapered staff, the top end of your rod secreted inside it, no-one will guess that you are actually going fishing – unless your broad grin gives the game away.

Undoubtedly foreshortened by the artist, this engraving shows a rod of the period with three sections and a loop at the tip.

Fishing Line

Making your own fishing line is almost as labour intensive, and here the starting point is a bunch of high quality long hairs from the tail of a white horse. (We learn in later writings that the horse should be a stallion or a gelding, as mares urinate on their own tails and weaken the hairs.) Divide this bunch into six equal parts and put one bunch aside to use as tippet. The other five must be dyed in various colours for use in particular seasons and water conditions – green for summer fishing, yellow for the autumn, russet for winter, brown for dark and sluggish water, and tawny 'for these waters that ben hethy or morysh' (heathy or marshy). Dame Juliana provides the recipes and instructions for achieving these colours, using such ingredients as copper, beer, walnut juice and soot.

Even the best individual horsehair has a test strength of little more than 1lb (0.5kg), so she then goes on to explain how to twist and plait the hairs together to make sections of line (later known as links) of sufficient strength, using a device that you can make at home with a little help from the blacksmith. She even prescribes the knots – the water knot and the duchess knot – that you should use to join the links together to create the right length of line. 'Thus shall your lynes be fayre and fyne, and also right sure for any maner of fysshe.'

Although fishing reels had been in use in China for many centuries, they did not appear in England until the mid 1600s, so the line, somewhat longer than the rod itself, was attached directly to the loop at the end of the rod. Playing a big fish on an outfit like this would certainly teach you to keep the rod tip up!

Dame Juliana includes an illustration of a device for making horsehair lines.

The Hooks

Like every other item of tackle, hooks are homemade, and Dame Juliana admits that '...the moste subtill and hardest craft in makyng your harneys [tackle], is for to make your hookes'. She lists the tools that the would-be hook maker needs and then gives a step-by-step account of the process. This involves heating a needle in a fire to make it workable, raising a barb with a strong knife, filing the point, tempering the needle again in the fire before bending it to shape, and then hammering the tail of the hook flat and filing it smooth. Finally the hook is made red hot and quenched in water to make it hard and strong.

Hooks of different sizes are made by choosing needles, or even nails, of the appropriate size, and the strength of the tippet must suit the size of the hook and the fish you are angling for – a single hair for the minnow, two for the growing roach, three for the dace and the great roach, four for the perch, six for the bream and the eel, and nine for the trout, grayling and barbel. The great trout requires twelve hairs, and the salmon fifteen. Horsehair gives way to a wire trace when it comes to the pike.

Anglers had to make their own hooks from needles of various sizes using fairly simple tools.

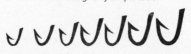

Palmer-Worm

YEAR: 1600s   **FLY TYER:** Anon.   **LOCATION:** England

The Original Recipe

Hook
Handmade from a bent and tempered
needle, with a hand-cut barb

Thread
Red silk

Body
Deep red mohair

Palmered hackle
Brown red cock's hackle

Rib (optional)
Gold wire or gold tinsel

Head
Black silk

'In March or April, if the Weather be dark, or a little windy or cloudy, the best Fishing is with the Palmer-Worm, which, with the May-Fly, are the Ground of all Fly-Angling.' So said the English physician and author Richard Brookes in his book *The Art of Angling, Rock and Sea Fishing*, written in 1740. This fly was already well established at the time and, in a variety of modern forms, it remains a 'go to' fly for trout anglers around the world.

ENTOMOLOGY OR ETYMOLOGY?

The first recorded use of the word 'palmer' appears in 1300, meaning a pilgrim returning from the Holy Land carrying a palm leaf, often folded in the form of a cross, as a token of the journey he had made. It later came to mean any pilgrim, of which there were many in Europe in the Middle Ages, making their way between the shrines and holy places. By the 1500s the term was being applied to hairy caterpillars that travel in groups, wander in all directions and devour everything in their path. After fly tyers made imitations of the palmer, or palmer-worm, by winding the hackle in open spiral wraps around the body of the fly to re-create the bristling hairs, the term 'palmer' eventually came to refer not only to the fly but also to this form of hackle. The palmered hackle is used on a vast array of wet and dry flies today.

Gregarious, ravenous, and apparently aimless, the 'palmer' hairy caterpillar took its name from the pilgrims who wandered throughout Europe in the Middle Ages. The palmered hackle is derived from this.

In the 15th and 16th centuries flies were already being tied to represent not only flying insects but also terrestrials such as ants and beetles. Walton, writing in 1653, says that there are too many flies to name 'and, yet, I will exercise your promised patience by saying a little of the caterpillar, or the palmer-fly or worm'.

Hairy caterpillars, which frequently fall into rivers and lakes from overhanging branches, were a natural choice for the fly tyer, and the Palmer-Worm proved to be deadly, tied in a wide range of colours, although Walton's contemporary, Thomas Barker, also published in 1653, seems to have had a preference for black:

The Mysterious Author

Although much less is known about Richard Brookes than his more famous seventeenth-century predecessor Izaak Walton (see page 23), author of *The Compleat Angler*, the little information we have points to an interesting character. *The Art of Angling, Rock and Sea Fishing, with the Natural History of River, Pond, and Sea Fish* was first published in 1740, and was still in print 50 years later. The frontispiece of that later edition is shown here. Despite its success, it was his only book on the subject of fishing. He was a physician by trade, and his other works included the *History of the Most Remarkable Pestilential Distempers* (1721) and the six-volume work *A System of Natural History* (1763). From the preface of the latter, we know that he travelled to both America and Africa – an unusual achievement for someone in that age. In 1724, he also translated *The Natural History of Chocolate*, from the French *Histoire Naturelle du Cacao et du Sucre* (published in 1719).

The frontispiece of Richard Brookes's book, originally published in 1740, shows a Palmer in the top-right corner. The terms 'drake' and 'dun' were used to refer to mayflies and caddis, or sedge, flies repectively.

'Let us begin to Angle in March with the Flie: If the weather prove Windie, or Cloudie, there are severall kindes of Palmers that are good for that time.

First, a black Palmer ribbed with silver: the second, a black Palmer with an Orange-tauny body: thirdly, a black Palmer, with the body made all of black: fourthly, a red Palmer ribbed with gold, and a red hackle mixed with Orange cruel; these Flies serve all the year long morning and evening, windie and cloudie'.

Two hundred years later, the virtues of this fly were still being extolled. In his *Handbook of Angling*, published in 1848, Edward Fitzgibbon lists six variations on the 'palmer-hackle' as he calls it, including a red hackle wrapped over peacock herl. He advises the angler to use small and 'sober' patterns when the water is clear and low, but to choose larger and more conspicuously coloured versions 'when used on waters that are disturbed, and the day is dark'.

Francis H. Buzzacott's *Complete Sportsman's Encyclopedia*, published in 1913, lists 24 different palmer colour combinations but today only a few basic palmer patterns are still in use. The best known of these is the Soldier Palmer – a red body with a red/brown palmered hackle – and it probably looks very similar to the palmer flies of 400 years ago.

'As they are meant to represent the larvae or caterpillars of flies, as well as some of the insects themselves, it is very evident that their size and colours may be varied to infinity.' **Delaborde P. Blaine, quoted in *Handbook of Angling*, Edward Fitzgibbon, 1848**

The first colour plate in Mary Orvis *Marbury's* Favorite Flies and Their Histories *depicts several palmers, including the red-jacketed Soldier Palmer shown here. It remains a popular fly.*

DESCENDANTS OF THE PALMER-WORM

The question of whether the original Palmer-Worm was a wet fly or a dry fly is a moot one, as the distinction was not made at the time. All flies were designed to float when first cast, but all would eventually sink. A fly could be dried and returned to the surface or could be deliberately, and often very effectively, fished slightly under the water. Until the introduction of the reel, the line – seldom longer than 9ft (2.7m) – was attached to the tip of the rod, so the angler could suspend the fly where he or she wished but had to be extremely subtle to avoid spooking the fish.

When the palmer migrated to the USA, however, it underwent an interesting metamorphosis and became most definitely a wet fly. Tied with a body of wool or chenille, and with a generally shorter palmered hackle, it sprouted a red woollen tail to emulate the caterpillar known in the southern states as the woolly worm, and this fly is still very popular, often with a wire-wound body or a bead head to help it sink. Said to have originated in the Ozarks of Missouri and Arkansas in the 1920s as a bass fly, the Woolly Worm was made popular by the Montana fly tyer Don Martinez in the 1950s. (He was, incidentally, one of the founders of the The Izaak Walton League, the environmental organisation that was largely responsible for the introduction of the US Clean Water Act in 1972.)

In yet another incarnation, the palmer also became the famous Woolly Bugger, similarly tied with a chenille body and a short, stiff hackle, but now with a long tail (and sometimes an underbody) of marabou feather. The soft fibres undulate as the fly is stripped gently through the water, giving a very lifelike impression of a leech, but this fly can do much more than that. In their many variations – and there are hundreds – both the Woolly Worm and the Woolly Bugger can emulate anything from a leech to a dragonfly or damsel nymph, a stonefly, or small fry.

Despite its efficacy, some fly fishing purists don't consider the Woolly Bugger to be a fly at all, and when it is seen fished under a strike indicator with split shot on the line one can understand their point of view. The British version of the fly, often tied with a lead wire underbody, dumbbell eyes and ice chenille, is known as a Dog Nobbler. It has been known to take sea trout in the ocean as well as lake pike.

This brown trout fell to the ever-popular Woolly Bugger on the Muleshoe Bend of the Firehole River in Yellowstone National Park, Montana.

Salmon on the Dry

Edward R. Hewitt was one of the first to champion the dry fly – and his Bi-Visible in particular – for salmon fishing. He and others, such as M.L. LaBranche, had considerable success using the method for Atlantic salmon in the 1920s, and West Coast anglers tried similar methods for steelhead and Pacific salmon at that time, but it didn't catch on until the 1930s, influenced largely by Lee Wulff.

In 1946, at the age of 80, E.R. Hewitt was still working and inventing in his laboratory on the third floor of his New York mansion on Gramercy Park. Among others, he held patents on the felt-soled wading shoe, an interchangeable fly reel and a grease that 'floats, softens, polishes and preserves' fishing line.

THE PALMER LIVES ON

As if such famous offspring were not enough, the palmer also lives on as a dry fly. The Bi-Visible was first brought to the attention of anglers in 1926 by the American inventor, chemist, engineer, naturalist and keen angler Edward Ringwood Hewitt in his book *Telling on the Trout*. The fly was designed to solve a fundamental problem, namely that trout respond better to a dark colour on the water's surface but anglers can't see a dark fly on the water, especially in low light. The majority of the hackle of the Bi-Visible is dark, usually brown, ginger or black, while the hackle at the head is white, or at least pale, making it visible to both the predator and the prey. The hackles are tied on a smooth thread base only, making the fly very light, and some tyers add a hackle tail. Generally fished on the surface as a traditional dry fly, skated or on a dead drift, the Bi-Visible can also be fished just below the surface as a nymph.

Green Drake

YEAR: 1676   **FLY TYER:** Charles Cotton   **LOCATION:** Derbyshire, England

The Original Recipe

Hook
Handmade from a bent and tempered needle, with a hand-cut barb

Thread
Yellow silk

Tail
Long hairs of sables or fitchet

Body
Camel hair, bright bear hair, soft hog's down and yellow camlet

Ribbing
Yellow silk waxed with green wax

Wings
White grey feather of a mallard, dyed yellow

Izaak Walton's The *Compleat Angler* is probably the best known angling book of all time, but from the fly fisher's perspective it is the contribution of his close friend Charles Cotton, included in the fifth edition of the book in 1676, that marks the greatest progress in fly tying. Cotton was one of a number of anglers and writers who had begun to show a great deal more attention to the detail of the natural insects and to incorporate their observations in their artificial flies.

Like Izaak Walton, Charles Cotton was a Royalist, and after the victory of the Parliamentarians that ended the English Civil War in 1651 he retired to the countryside to write and pursue his sporting interests.

BARKER'S CONTRIBUTION

Originally published in 1653, Walton's angling classic has been through more reprints that any other book in the English language with the exception of the Bible and the Book of Common Prayer. Very little of his book deals with fly fishing or fly tying, and what there is is largely taken, with acknowledgement, from Thomas Barker's *The Art of Angling*, published in London two years earlier.

Barker, who gives one of the first detailed step-by-step descriptions of how to tie a fly, was also the first to mention the process that we would call dubbing, saying, 'If you make the grounds of Hogs-wooll, sandy, black or white; or the wooll of a Bear, or of a two year old red Bullock: you must work all these grounds upon a waxed silk…'

THE FIFTH EDITION

At Walton's request, Charles Cotton contributed a second section to the 1676 edition of *The Compleat Angler* consisting of 12 chapters on *How to Angle for a Trout or Grayling in a Clear Stream*. This is almost entirely about fly fishing and it is filled with information about rods and line, and about fishing with natural and artificial flies. He also provides instructions on how to tie more than 60 flies specific to the months of the year, rather as Dame Juliana had done. Cotton makes no claim to have invented these flies himself and it is likely that they come from other fly tyers and from different parts of the country. What makes his text remarkable is the detail with which he describes

*'I confess, no direction can be given to make a man of a dull capacity able to make a fly well.… But to see a fly made by an artist in that kind, is the best teaching to make it'. **Izaak Walton***

the life cycle, behaviour and appearance of the insects themselves. For example, he devotes several hundred words to the green drake (the large European *Ephemera danica*) before explaining how to tie an artificial replica, including how to dye mallard feathers to create the wings.

TYING THE GREEN DRAKE

The green drake in England (Ephemera danica) is much paler than the green drake (Ephemera guttulata) or Western green drake (Drunella grandis / doddsii) in the USA, where Cotton's fly would be closer to a Sulphur Dun or Light Cahill.

Having given general directions on how to tie winged flies (as opposed to hackle, or palmer, flies) Charles Cotton gives no specific instructions for tying this particular fly, but he does provide a list of ingredients and his dubbing is very detailed. He recommends a mixture of camel hair, 'bright' bear hair, soft down combed from a hog's bristles, and yellow camlet, which was a soft fabric made of goat's hair and silk. (The range of materials – some of them extremely specific – used in the tying of Cotton's flies is far greater than that of other writers at that time.) The long body is dubbed with this and then ribbed with yellow silk that has been rubbed with green wax. The tail whisks are long hairs from a sable or fitchet (members of the marten family), and the wings are a bundle of light mallard feather fibres dyed yellow.

There is no mention of a hackle. Although palmers, with their spirally wound hackle, were occasionally given wings, winged flies would not gain a collar hackle until the 19th century.

MODERN DUBBING

Barker mentioned the process of dubbing, but at that time the word itself was being applied broadly to mean winding any material around the hook shank, or even tying a fly on a hook in general. Charles Cotton, however, little more than 20 years later, is clearly using the word in its modern sense: 'And then take your dubbing which is to make the body of your fly, as much as you think convenient, and holding it lightly, with your hook, betwixt the finger and thumb of your left hand, take your silk with the right, and twisting it betwixt the finger and thumb of that hand, the dubbing will spin itself about the silk...'

Interestingly, Cotton recommends that once a winged fly is finished the tyer should 'with the point of a needle, raise up the dubbing gently from the warp,' presumably to give an impression of legs. It's an instruction that we'll hear again applied to the Hare's Ear Nymph 200 years later.

In some copies of the fifth edition of *The Compleat Angler,* a third part, written by Robert Venables and entitled *The Experienced Angler*, was included. Although his entomology may not have been up to much ('…the stone-fly, by some called the May-fly, which is bred of the water cricket'), he was the first to discuss the pros and cons of upstream fishing. He advised the angler to match the hatch and to tie flies 'by sight' rather than following written instructions, since many flies have several names and many names refer to several flies.

Venables is noteworthy for several innovations, one of the most remarkable being the design of a fly that would swim upside down in the water, with the hook uppermost. It's a theme that returns in the 20th century in the form of the upside-down parachute dry fly and the Clouser Minnow. Venables was clearly proud of his invention, as it appears twice on the frontispiece of his book. He was also the first to suggest adding weight to the shank of the hook to get the fly down deep. He suggested this trick for a caddis larva pattern and gave instructions for a sink and draw retrieve that showed he had been observing the natural.

He also mentions fly fishing for a wider range of fish than just the usual suspects: 'In general, all sorts of flies are very good in their season, for such fish as will rise at the fly, viz. Salmon, Trout, Umber, Grayling, Bleak, Chevin [chub], Roach, Dace, &c'. He also tells us that some 'angle for Bream and Pike with artificial flies, but I judge the labour lost…' Many a modern pike angler would disagree with that last part, but the last 20 years have seen a resurgence in fly fishing for many freshwater species that have long been thought of as the quarry of the bait fisher only.

The frontispiece from Venables's tract, published in 1660, shows rods that differ little in appearance from that of 1496, but the materials used for rod making had begun to change, and a reel, or "winder," has entered the picture.

THE STATE OF THE ART IN 1800

*T*he contents of an angler's fly box in 1800 would not have looked greatly different from that of Izaak Walton's, or even Dame Juliana's, time. Changes in fly tying techniques, the introduction of some new materials and a greater focus on the living insects meant that flies were more refined and a little more lifelike, but the patterns were broadly the same. Similarly, had we looked at the state of angling technology in 1600 or 1700 we would have seen very few advances on the rods, lines and hooks of the 15th century. However, in the course of the 18th century the evolution of fishing equipment finally began to accelerate.

Rods

One of the themes of rods in the second half of the 1700s is diversification. Prior to that time an angler would generally use the same rod – possibly with different thicknesses of line – for fly fishing, float fishing or trolling. Now the fly rod was becoming a thing in its own right and different lengths of rod started to be used for different kinds of fly fishing, from a 12ft (3.7m) trout rod to a 17ft (5m) salmon rod.

This entailed the use of a wider variety of woods and the tailoring of the rod to the individual needs of the angler, and rod making was becoming increasingly specialised. In the early 1600s there were very few craftsmen making fishing rods for sale, but by the mid 1700s very few anglers were making their own. There was

'…to the shore you gaily drag your unresisting prize.' This engraving shows an angler handlining a fish to the bank. Without a reel, one had to hope the prize was indeed unresisting.

even a growing export trade in rods, with some London makers shipping their goods as far afield as the Caribbean, New England and Newfoundland. In turn, South and North America provided exotic woods such as lancewood and the stiff, dense and strong hickory wood that were gradually replacing the traditional hazel and yew for upper sections. Ash, deal and willow remained the woods of choice for bottom sections.

Although jointed rods had been around since Dame Juliana's day, rod sections were generally still spliced together because no form of joint had yet been developed that was neither too heavy nor too fragile. It was also believed, probably quite rightly, that the joints affected the action of the rod.

Rod tips, which had to be springy in order to play a fish without breaking the line or – all too commonly – the tip of the rod itself, continued to be made of 'whalebone' throughout the 1700s, as they had been since the early 1600s. However, towards the end of the century a new strong and flexible wood made its appearance from the East Indies. Slim bamboo cane, used whole, was found to make a good salmon rod tip, and makers experimented with thicker sections for lower parts of the rod, but it was as split cane that it would change the face of fly fishing in the following century.

Baleen

The 'whalebone' used for rod tips in the 17th and 18th centuries was not actually bone but a substance called baleen. Baleen whales, which include the blue whale, the minke whale and the humpback, have no teeth and instead have a comb-like arrangement of fringed baleen plates (made of keratin, like our fingernails) that hang from the upper jaw. Baleen whales are filter feeders, taking vast quantities of water into their mouths and then forcing the water out through the baleen plates to sieve out the food items, which may be tiny krill or larger baitfish. A by-product of the whaling industry, baleen was used for a wide range of purposes, from corset stays to umbrella ribs, well into the 20th century, eventually being replaced by plastics and other synthetic materials.

This is the baleen of a grey whale, which can consume up to 1.5 tonnes of food a day.

Rod Rings

The 16th-century rod had a horsehair loop spliced to its tip, and the fishing line, also of horsehair, was attached to this. This meant that the line could only be slightly longer than the rod itself, and the loop was gradually replaced by an iron ring through which a greater length of 'running line' could pass, the spare line lying coiled at the angler's feet until it was needed to play a fish. When the line was under tension the rod would bend and cause the line to run through the end ring at a sharp angle, so in the 1700s intermediate rod rings were introduced, particularly on salmon rods, spreading the bending load along the length of the rod and improving the angle at the tip. The downside of these was an increased number of obstacles for the knotted horsehair to pass through, and because the rings were simply spiked into the rod they would frequently pull out.

Landing a good-sized fish in the 17th century, with neither a reel nor rod rings, took skill and more than a little luck.

Reels

Although reels are mentioned by both Barker (1651) and Venables (1662), referring to them as a winder and a winch respectively, they seem only to have been used by fishers of pike and salmon until the 18th century, and then largely as a means of storing line rather than for playing the fish. They were generally bulky and fairly crude, but by the early 1700s a range of more sophisticated brass reels – manufactured for the growing number of anglers at the time – was available and becoming increasingly popular.

Then came a surprising detour. The simple single-action reel of the time had a wide and shallow spool that made retrieving the line a slow process. One might expect the solution to

'The next way of angling is with a troll for the Pike, which is very delightful; you may buy your troll ready made, therefore I shall not trouble myself to describe it, only let it have a winch to wind it up withall.'
Venables, *The Experienced Angler*, 1662

This brass reel from the late 1700s has a spike fitting to attach it to the rod and a very narrow arbour that made it hard to recover line quickly.

lie in the development of a large arbour reel, but no – in that age of industry and mechanisation, the much more complex multiplier reel came into being instead. In the words of angling's most comprehensive historian, Andrew Herd (to whom we are deeply indebted), it was 'a case of an idea made metal before its time'. Brass, for all its great qualities, is not the ideal material for small gears that are working to control a 9kg (20lb) salmon.

Nonetheless their use became widespread – and just in time to store the greater lengths of line made possible by mechanisation as the Industrial Revolution got under way.

Line

Horsehair remained the staple material for fishing line throughout the 18th century, but the problems posed by the difficulty of creating continuous lengths and by having knots all along the line were largely overcome in the last quarter of the century. The mechanisation of textiles manufacturing was at the heart of the Industrial Revolution, and a mechanical means of weaving horsehairs together was soon developed,

creating continuous, tapered, knotless line that, even though the tips of the hairs stuck out slightly and gave it a slightly spiky surface texture, would slide through the rod rings more easily than the knotted line.

Attempts were made to alleviate some of the disadvantages of horsehair line – such as its stiffness and its memory, especially when stored on a narrow spool – by adding silk to the mix, but this added water retention to the list. Silk did, however hold the key to great improvements that would take place the following century.

Hooks

By the mid 1700s the availability of high quality steel had made it possible to produce much stronger, lighter and more durable hooks, and before the end of the century they were being mass produced. Although there are examples of eyed hooks from Roman times, all hooks in the 18th century were still eyeless and had to be whipped to the horsehair. It would take another 50 years, even finer steel and a change in attitude before they would catch on.

The manufacture of horse hair lines improved in the 18th century with the advent of mechanised spinning methods.

Blae and Black

YEAR: 1800   **FLY TYER:** Anon.   **LOCATION:** Scotland

The Original Recipe

Hook
Down-eyed wet fly hook
#10–#14 (originally eyeless)

Ribbing
Round or half-round silver tinsel

Thread
Black tying silk

Hackle
Black hen hackle

Tail
Golden pheasant tippet

Wing
Matching slips of grey duck quill

Body
Black tying silk

Head
Varnished black tying silk

The origins of the Blae and Black are unknown, but it is an early member of the Scottish loch trout fly family. It is probably taken by trout as an emerging or drowned black midge, or chironomid, that goes by the same name in Scotland, but the pattern may have been first tied in Ireland, where the midge is a called a duck fly. Drab though it may be, the Blae and Black is a popular fly on the lakes of both countries in late March and early April when these large midges are hatching.

DUCK FLY PATTERNS

Hatches on the Scottish lochs and the loughs of western Ireland can be spectacular, and there is a large number of patterns that work well for the brown trout at this time, the majority of them being dark winged flies tied similarly to the Blae and Black. These include the Connemara Black, Watson's Fancy, Mallard and Claret, Peter Ross, Fiery Brown and Claret Dabbler. The well-known Black Pennell, effectively a Blae and Black without the grey wing, is another related pattern. The Scottish word blae means slate blue / grey, and here refers to the colour of the fly's wings, which are of grey duck or starling feather. (The phrase 'black and blue' was probably originally 'black and blae', bruising being more commonly slate coloured than blue.)

FISHING METHODS

In addition to casting from the shore in well-chosen locations, loch style fishing is done from a boat set to drift broadsides to the wind with the anglers casting down or across the wind. Typically three flies will be fished on a floating or intermediate sinking line and the Blae and Black is usually the 'bob' fly, positioned on the dropper closest to the rod. The flies are fished sub-surface with a slow figure-of-eight retrieval.

As well as being effective on still waters, the Blae and Black and other loch flies are fished in larger sizes, up to a #6, on the rivers of Ireland and throughout the UK for sea trout, dollaghan (the large brown trout of the Irish Lough Neagh river system) and even salmon.

Midge hatches in Ireland and Scotland in the spring can be so prolific that the water appears to have a cloud of smoke above it. On the Irish loughs the duck flies generally hatch from 'duck holes', silt-bottomed depressions in the lake bed.

Ogden's Fancy

YEAR: 1840   **FLY TYER:** James Ogden   **LOCATION:** Cheltenham, England

The Original Recipe

Hook
Light wire, #10–#12
(originally eyeless)

Thread
Yellow silk

Body
Yellow silk waxed with white wax

Tag
Gold tinsel

Tail
Red cock's hackle

Wings
Bright starling wing slips

Head
Yellow silk waxed with white wax

Hackle
Bright red cock's hackle with
black root and centre

'Since I brought this fly out, it has become a great favourite with those anglers who use a dry fly, it having all the properties of floating well. It is also very attractive when thrown over a rising fish, not allowing it to drag, which is the grand secret of using floating flies.' These words, referring to a fly – rarely, if ever, tied now – called Ogden's Fancy, were written by James Ogden in his book *Ogden On Fly Tying*, first published in 1879, and if the invention of the dry fly can be laid at the door of any one man, he is that man.

James Ogden's experiments and creativity in the first half of the 19th century led to the development of imitative and extremely effective fly patterns that would continue to float on the surface cast after cast. They were to revolutionise fly fishing – and ultimately to polarise the fly-fishing community – by the end of the 1800s.

Ever the promoter, James Ogden poses on his patent creel, an 8ft (2.4m) Multum in Parvo rod in his hand, his spring-folding landing net at this feet, and a fly book beside him revealing a selection of his floating flies.

Ogden was certainly not the first to note that when trout were taking flies on the surface the angler's best chance of hooking a fish came on the first cast, before the fly became waterlogged, but he was single minded in acting upon this observation. He began working with buoyant materials such as straw and cork for the bodies – which others had done before – probably as early as the 1830s and he was one of the principal forces behind the evolution of the hackled dry fly. He later claimed to have been fishing with his dry flies since 1840, and his floating patterns were certainly being sold by his own fishing tackle business in Cheltenham in the 1850s, but his greatest PR coup came in 1865.

'The wheelings of the black and blue gnats, in sunny calms and clear waters – the trotting of the stone fly, and the majestic floating of the green drake – overmatch the craftsman's art. Nature reigns there supreme, when her own works only can avail the flyfisher. The first cast of his artificials comes the nearest; they float for an instant and oft flatter him with a rise, or by chance a fish, but in a cast or two more they are disfigured, dishevelled, and drowned, and so must continue during his sport.' **Francis M. Walbran in Michael Theakston's *British Angling Flies* (1883)**

Dry Fly or Dry *Fly*?

The term 'dry fly' underwent a very significant change of meaning in the mid 1800s. From the very birth of the sport, any fly angler knew that when a fly was first cast it would tend to stay on the surface, but that it – and the line – would soon absorb water and sink. This wasn't a problem if the fish were feeding subsurface, but the angler who wanted to present the fly to rising fish would then have to keep the rod up and the line taut or else replace the fly with one that wasn't yet wet.

G.P.R. Pulman, in his *Vade-Mecum of Fly-Fishing for Trout*, published in 1841, presents the case very clearly: 'Impelled by some peculiarity of the atmosphere, or by some other cause…the fish have come close to the surface to watch for their prey, which can thus be easily seized as the victims float along, without further trouble on the part of the fish than gently lifting their mouths above the water. Now, the angler's

fly is wet and heavy, and, thrown from the other side, has a certain weight of line in addition. So, as it is not in the nature of things that this soaked artificial fly can swim upon the surface as the natural ones do, it follows the alternative and sinks below the rising fish, the notice of which it entirely escapes, because they happen just then to be looking upwards for the materials of their meal. Let a dry fly be substituted for the wet one, the line switched a few times through the air to throw off its super-abundant moisture, a judicious cast made just above the rising fish, and the fly allowed to float towards and over them, and the chances are ten to one that it will be seized as readily as a living insect.'

It is clear that 'Let a dry fly be substituted for the wet one' means simply replacing the fly, not putting on a different kind of fly, but that meaning was soon to be altered.

Although it was originally tied as a dry fly, we also owe Ogden for the Invicta, a classic hatching or egg-laying sedge pattern that has remained popular with wet fly anglers for well over a century, both on still waters and for sea trout.

A GAME CHANGER

James Ogden (1803–1880) was brought up in Derbyshire where he learnt to fish wet flies on the River Wye with his father, and after moving to Cheltenham he returned frequently to fish his home waters. In 1864 he was staying at an inn called The Peacock, at Rowsley, close to the confluence of the rivers Wye and Derwent and just a few miles from Haddon Hall, country home of the Duke of Rutland (whose emblem, incidentally, is a male peacock). The Wye, which runs through the Haddon estate, was famous for its hatch of drakes, during which anglers would cast live mayflies and catch huge numbers of trout. While at the inn, Ogden was approached by Robert Nesfield, the Duke's steward, who was looking for a way to maintain the sport fishing on the estate waters while reducing the size of the catch, and he asked Ogden whether his dry flies would catch trout even during the hatch, a feat that the local anglers considered impossible. Ogden confidently accepted the challenge, as well as an invitation to return the following June in time for the hatch.

On 5 June, 1865, Ogden was duly stationed on the River Wye, rod in hand and equipped with a 'dry' mayfly. Word of the challenge had spread, and an enthusiastic band of spectators watched from the nearby bridge. As Ogden recounts, 'After well soaking my cast, and testing it, I put on one of my artificial drakes, which looked very tempting dressed as follows: a straw body, ribbed with red silk well waxed; tail, three strands of hen pheasant tail feather; hackle, a pale buff with brown centre, rather short in

At Junction Pool, near Rowsley, the Derbyshire Wye flows in from the left to join the River Derwent. Together these waters provide some of the best dry fly fishing in the country.

fibre; wings, upright, taken from the wood or summer duck. I made a cast to the fish I first saw rise; my fly had scarcely touched the water, when it was taken'. Indeed, one of the on-lookers shouted that he must be using a live drake, as it had alighted on the water 'like the natural fly'.

Ogden proceeded to catch nine good fish and then waded into the water (with the steward's permis-sion, as wading was forbidden on the Haddon stretch and still is) to cast to a fish that was rising in mid river. Having hooked it, he found his foot stuck in the silt of the riverbed and he toppled backwards into the water, dropping his rod in the process, but he managed to land the trout before retiring to the inn for a change of clothes. His point had been made, and, as Ogden tells us, a member of his audience called out, 'If he hadn't fell in, he'd a killed every fish in the water!'

When he returned to the same spot the next morning to meet up with the steward, Ogden found himself very unpopular with a group of local anglers. He decided against fishing there again and said as much to the steward, who replied, 'Never mind, Ogden; you have carried out my wish-es, and from this morning I have prohibited all natural fly fishing. If they cannot kill with the artificial, they shall not with the live fly.' This was the very first introduction of a 'dry fly only' rule, one that would soon be applied to many of the chalk streams of southern England and far beyond.

ALL-ROUNDER

As well as being a fine angler and an accomplished fly dresser, James Ogden was a great inventor with an eye for a business opportunity, and he had an impact on aspects of fishing far beyond just flies. He designed and sold, both through his tackle shop in Cheltenham and by mail order, the Ogden's Noted Seat Basket (a wicker creel that provided a comfortable seat for the angler), Ogden's Spring Folding Landing Net (a long-handled folding net that could be assembled one-handed with a flick of the wrist) and a minnow-pattern spinner called the Devil Killer, of which he was

The Tying of Ogden's Fancy

'My mode of dressing it is as follows: body of bright yellow silk waxed with white wax, wrapping down evenly from the shoulder to the tail. Avoid making the body too long. Make a short tag with two or three wraps of fine gold tinsel round the bare hook, then tie in three strands of a red cock's hackle for tails, not covering the tag of gold, as it is a great attraction to the fly. Cut off the tying silk after securing it neatly; wax a fresh length of the yellow silk, set in at the head, and tie in the wings, which should be broad and taken from a bright starling wing feather. Set them on very upright. For legs, a bright red cock's hackle with a black root, and tapering to a point. If the hackle has a strip of black up the centre, so much the better, and the more killing the fly. Tie the hackle in close up behind the wings, and wrap the clean waxed silk down the body to the tail. Take the tip of the hackle in the tweezers, put two turns at the shoulder close up behind the wings, and rib the hackle down the body as close together as it will allow for it to

reach the tag. Before taking the tweezers off tie in the tip of the hackle neatly with one wrap and two knots. Be particular not to cover the tag. Cut out any stray fibres that will not lay even.' *Ogden on Fly Tying*, 1887.

Held in the jaws of his Improved Fly Vice, one of Ogden's upwinged dry flies is in the process of having its collar hackle wound.

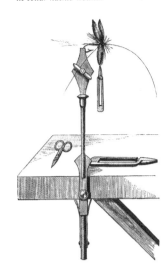

extremely proud. One of his greatest innovations, however, was the introduction of the short fly fishing rod. Traditional rods at the time were up to 16ft (4.9m) long, while his 'Multum in Parvo' (much in little) range included rods as short as 8.5ft (2.6m). These fundamentally altered the nature of fly casting and facilitated the use of the false cast, enabling the angler to 'crack off' the excess moisture and keep the line and the dry fly floating.

'It is well known that I am the inventor of Floating Flies, the Seat Basket, and the Spring-Folding Landing Net, which is so conveniently carried on the basket strap; also the celebrated Devil Killers, which have proved so deadly that they have been prohibited on many streams.' **James Ogden,**
Ogden on Fly Tying (1887)

Stewart Black Spider

YEAR: 1857   **FLY TYER:** W.C. Stewart   **LOCATION:** East Lothian, Scotland

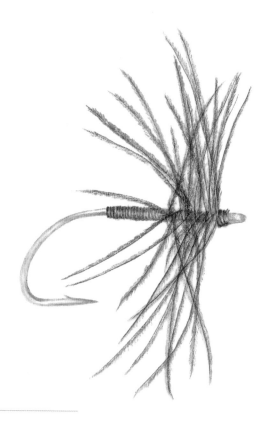

The Original Recipe

Hook
Standard or short-shank wet fly
hook #12–#20 (originally eyeless)

Body and head
Waxed dark brown thread

Thread
Dark brown

Hackle
Soft starling body feather

'The artificial flies in common use may be divided into two classes. There is first the winged fly, which alone, properly speaking, merits the appellation; and there is the palmer hackle or spider, by which last name we mean to call it, believing that if it resembles anything in the insect tribe, it is a spider. As a means of capturing trout, we rank them higher than the winged imitations.' W.C. Stewart was writing in 1857, and his name is commonly associated with the inception of the soft-hackle fly in general and the Black Spider in particular.

RETURN OF THE PALMER

As we have already seen, the palmer hackle was in use in the form of the Palmer-Worm back in the 1600s, so what makes Stewart's flies (he also gave instructions for tying the Dun Spider and the Red Spider) so different? Well, in the first place, this is not a bulky fly with a solid underbody. The body of Stewart's spider is made solely of thread and covers two-thirds of the hook shank at most. Secondly, whereas the hackle of the palmer-worm is stiff and spiky and runs the full length of the hook, Stewart's long hackle fibres are soft, sparse, and are wrapped only part way down the shank, making this a very different kind of fly.

According to Mary Orivis Marbury, 'The Spider Hackle is a favorite pattern with Mr W.C. Prime [whose dressing it is], who considers its action upon the water extremely lifelike.'

ORIGINS

Stewart himself never made any claim to have invented the fly and attributes it to the ghillie with whom he fished, referring to him as 'the celebrated James Baillie, considered by all who knew him the ablest fly-fisher in Scotland'. Baillie was a professional fly fisher, not only acting as a ghillie but also supporting his family through the sale of the fish that he caught – which Stewart tells us amounted to between 12lb (5kg) and 14lb (6kg) of fish each day he fished – and the fact that he used these spider-style flies speaks volumes.

However, nor was Baillie the inventor of the spider. This style of fly came originally from the northern counties of England and the Borders, where it remains popular to this day, and the first written mention of them dates from the early 1800s, when John Swarbrick, a farmer from Austby in Wharfedale, wrote down a list of the local flies that included several of

these patterns. The list didn't make its way into print until 100 years later, but the flies clearly spread throughout the north of England and made their way into Scotland. Their popularity increased after the publication of Stewart's book *The Practical Angler*, and more so after the appearance in 1885 of T.E. Pritt's *Yorkshire Trout Flies*. This book was republished the next year as *North Country Flies*, the term by which these flies are still known.

THE SPIDER FAMILY

Pritt lists more than 60 flies in use in Yorkshire at the time and gives details of the materials needed for tying them as well as when and where to fish them. Some are winged flies, some have dubbed bodies, but many are these very sparsely tied spider-type patterns. Three that are still well respected are listed by him as the Dark Snipe, the Yellow Partridge and the Orange Partridge. These are now known as the Snipe and Purple, the Partridge and Yellow, and the Partridge and Orange, after the hackle and the thread used in each case.

The Bloas

Among his North Country flies, Pritt also includes a number that are called bloas. Some of these are winged and tailed, but most are sparsely hackled in a similar fashion to the spiders. Two in particular – the Waterhen Bloa and the Poult Bloa – are still commonly used. A poult is a young bird, in this case a young grouse (the word pullet has the same origin).

'Bloa' refers to the colour of the hackle and appears to be equivalent to the Scottish word 'blae', meaning slate blue/grey.

The grouse is one of many game birds whose feathers, in shades of dun, tan, brown, black and rust, are ideal for soft-hackled flies.

The reason for the great success of the spiders and their relatives, as agreed by Stewart, Pritt, Theakston, and many fishing authorities since, is the hackle, which constitutes the major part of the fly. On the palmer and the winged fly, the hackle was, and is, generally that of a cock, but Stewart had this to say: 'We...think the cock-hackle by no means deserving of so much attention as is bestowed upon it, being too stiff and wiry to represent the legs of an insect, and we prefer hen-hackles, or still better, the small feathers taken from the neck or outside of the wings of a variety of small birds,' and he goes on to explain why this is important.

This lovely illustration of trout and a grayling forms the frontispiece to the fifth edition of The Practical Angler or The Art of Trout-Fishing More Particularly Applied to Clear Water, *by W.C. Stewart.*

'When trout are well fed and become lazy, or where they are much fished for, and become shy, we have found spiders much more deadly than the most tempting winged fly that can be made. Nor is it necessary to go very much out of the way to seek a reason for this: the hook is better concealed, and if made of sufficiently soft materials, the water agitates the feathers, and gives them a life-like appearance, which has a wonderful effect, and is of itself a sufficient reason for trout preferring them...'

Stewart was one of the first to explain the efficacy of a fly in terms of the impression that it gave rather than its true-to-life accuracy, and Pritt took this theory even further. Both made the case that a perfect, but stiff, imitation was far less likely to be taken by a fish than was a fly that gives the general appearance of a drowned or crippled insect being tossed by the current. The soft hackle fibres identified by Stewart fulfilled this role admirably and, while looking exactly like nothing, could give an impression of the legs, wings or shucks of mayfly emergers, duns and spinners, gnats and midges, as well as various nymphs, when fished at different levels in the water column and even in the surface film.

'The great error of fly-fishing, as usually practised, and as recommended to be practised by books, is that the angler fishes down stream, whereas he should fish up.' **W.C. Stewart, The Practical Angler (1867)**

Mr Stewart tells us that 'Spiders dressed of very soft feathers are more suitable for fishing up than for fishing down, as, if drawn against the stream, it runs the fibres alongside of the hook, and all resemblance to an insect is destroyed.' That sounds like good sense, and who could take exception to that? Well, a great many anglers in southern England, it would seem, where down and across remained the standard wet fly presentation, even though Robert Venables had advocated upstream fishing back in 1662. Admittedly, the reason for that difference of opinion lies in part in the differences between northern and southern waters. Rivers in the south, fed by the chalk hills, tend to be slow and meandering as they make their way across relatively level terrain, whereas rain-fed rivers in the more mountainous north of England and southern Scotland can be fast and turbulent, calling for different flies and different methods of fishing them.

Comparing the qualities of feathers from various birds, Stewart writes, "…we consider the feathers taken from the cock starling the most valuable of all to the angler. They have a rich glossy black, which no other feathers possess, and we always use them in place of the black cock-hackle."

Stewart's main objection, however, was that any method other than what we would call a dead drift must appear unnatural. In his words, 'Having dismissed the idea that the angler can imitate the flight of a living fly along the surface of the water, we must suppose that trout take the artificial fly for a dead one, or one which has fairly got into the stream and lost all power of resisting. A feeble motion of the wings or legs would be the only attempt at escape which a live fly in such a case could make. What then must be the astonishment of the trout, when they see the tiny insect which they are accustomed to seize as it is carried by the current towards them, crossing the stream with the strength and agility of an otter? Is it not much more natural to throw the flies up, and let them come gently down as any real insect would do?'

DRESSING THE SPIDER

Even though spiders were clearly his favourite flies, Stewart continued to fish winged wet flies, and one of the reasons that he gave for this was the fragility of the soft hackle, which caused the fly to be wrecked fairly quickly when taken by a trout or grayling. However, he did find a way to give the fly greater durability. In his fly tying instructions, once the hackle feather – a black cock starling feather – is tied in place with the stem pointing toward the bend of the hook and trimmed off, he does something very innovative. 'What remains to be

done is the most critical part of the whole operation: still holding the hook between the forefinger and thumb of your left hand [Stewart did not use a vice], take the thread, lay it along the centre of the inside of the feather, and with the forefinger and thumb of your right hand twirl them round together till the feather is rolled round the thread; and in this state wrap it round the hook, taking care that a sufficient number of the fibres stick out to represent the legs…. This is a very rough and simple mode of dressing a spider, and does not make it so neat as if the feather were put on by a pair of nippers, but it is more natural-looking, and much more durable, as the feather is fastened on by the thread the whole way down.' It's a tip that many a fly tyer has applied to a whole range of flies ever since.

Another way to make the fly last longer is to tie on more hackle than the absolute minimum. In this way, as it becomes increasingly mauled by the teeth of fish and loses fibres, the fly steadily approaches the sparse ideal, which some tyers say should be as few as eight fibres, taking the spider theme very literally.

Stewart preferred sparse patterns, saying, 'The first of the accompanying flies is a spider, the second a fly dressed with dubbing, and the third a fly dressed with a hackle. The reader will observe that these flies are very light in the make; that there is not more dubbing than covers the thread; that the hackle is put on very sparingly; and that the dressing is not carried far down the hook.'

THE SOFT HACKLE LIVES ON

In the more than 200 years since John Swarbrick wrote his list of Wharfedale flies, the popularity of soft-hackled flies has repeatedly waxed and waned, but their simplicity and success has kept them alive. The great advocate of nymph fishing, G.E.M. Skues (see page 90), did much to revive interest in them, as did Leisenring and Hidy with their 'flymphs' (see pages 122–7) and, more recently, Sylvester Nemes (see page 185). Now, far from being a minor tributary, soft-hackled flies are part of the mainstream, as we shall see later, and the principles of the soft hackle are increasingly being applied to other, more complex, fly designs – including dry flies – to impart that pulsating vitality that so captured the imagination of W.C. Stewart.

'It is far more difficult to imitate a perfect insect and to afterwards impart to it a semblance of life in or on the water, than it is to produce something which is sufficiently near a resemblance of an imperfectly developed insect, struggling to attain the surface of the stream.' **Thomas Evan Pritt,** ***North-Country Flies*** **(1886)**

Greenwell's Glory

YEAR: 1854   **FLY TYER:** James Wright / William Greenwell   **LOCATION:** Roxburghshire, Scotland

The Original Recipe

Hook
Down eye wet fly #12–#16
(originally eyeless)

Thread
Primrose yellow silk

Ribbing
Fine silver wire

Hackle
Red and black hackle

Wing
Matching slips of starling
(originally blackbird) quill

Head
Varnished black silk

In his autobiography, *My Life as an Angler*, William Henderson wrote about some exceptional days of fishing on the Tweed, in the Scottish Borders, enjoyed by William Greenwell and James Wright: 'The work was chiefly done with flies dressed of feathers taken from the blackbird's wing, the bodies being formed of coch-y-bonddhu hackles. So deadly did these flies prove that they have been awarded the commemorative title of "Greenwell's Glory". In spring and early summer I invariably use one on my cast of flies, and with the exception of the March Brown have found none more successful.'

CANON'S INSPIRATION

The date was May 1854, William Greenwell was an archaeologist and a clergyman (he was appointed a canon at Durham Cathedral later that year), and his fishing companion, James Wright, was one of the greatest fly tyers of the time. The fly that bears Greenwell's name is said to have been born of a fruitless day when the fish were taking a fly that Greenwell didn't recognise. He went to James Wright, who lived nearby, with his idea for the fly that Henderson described – a blackbird feather wing, a red and black hackle, and a body of yellow silk. The following day he reportedly caught 32lb (14.5kg) of trout on the new fly, much to Wright's amazement. He repeated this performance the next day, and that evening his fellows anglers in the Durham Rangers Fishing Club, with whom he had travelled north, raised their glasses and wished 'Success to Greenwell's Glory'. It has since become one of the world's most famous patterns, representing a range of mayflies.

Although the original fly had wings of blackbird feather, other grey wing slips such as woodcock, starling and widgeon are now more commonly used.

MODERN VARIATIONS

At the time it was tied, dry fly fishing had barely taken off, so this was a wet fly, but its colour combination and essential qualities have graced many variations. The modern wet fly is generally tied with a pair of starling feather slip wings, waxed thread that gives it a slightly green hue, a thin gold wire rib and a furnace hackle. Some have a hackle fibre tail. There is also a wingless soft hackle version that Stewart would have approved of, as well as the dry Greenwell's and a parachute version (see Adams, page 102).

Lady Caroline

YEAR: 1875   **FLY TYER:** Geordie Shanks   **LOCATION:** Moray, Scotland

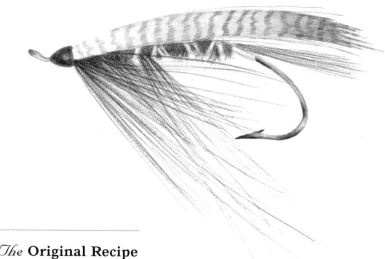

The Original Recipe

Hook
Black Spey hook, #4–#1/0
(originally eyeless)

Ribbing
Gold tinsel (narrow),
gold twist and silver twist

Thread
Black tying silk

Spey hackle
Blue-eared pheasant
(originally grey heron)

Tail
Golden pheasant red breast fibres

Throat hackle
Golden pheasant red breast

Body
Two parts brown Berlin wool
and one part olive green, dubbed

Wings
Two strips of mallard showing
brown points and light roots

When it comes to Scottish salmon fishing, few rivers have more history or mystique than the Spey. The highly identifiable style of salmon fly that evolved on that river in the early 19th century has proven to have a lasting appeal and still influences fly tyers today. The Lady Caroline, with its aristocratic origins, is one of a small number of Spey flies that continues to be used, unchanged, on both sides of the Atlantic.

SALMON ON THE FLY

References to fly fishing for salmon have popped up in the literature since Dame Juliana said that you may take a salmon with a dubbed fly 'but it is seldom seen', presumably because the tackle of the time wasn't up to the task of getting a fly out to a fish in a wide river nor of landing it once hooked.

In the 17th century Walton was not a great deal more positive, saying of the salmon '...he is very seldom observed to bite at a minnow, yet sometimes he will, and not usually at a fly...'. His contemporary, Thomas Barker was more optimistic about our chances and tells us more about the

Over 100 miles (160km) long, the River Spey, seen here at Blacksboat to the east of Inverness, rises in the Scottish Highlands and flows north-east through Abelour and Craigellachie to the Moray Firth.

Lady Caroline – Kelson's Instructions

Tail: Golden pheasant red breast, a few strands only

Body: Brown and olive-green Berlin wool mixed together in proportion of one part olive-green, two parts brown

Ribs: From separate starting points, of gold tinsel (narrow), gold twist, and silver twist, wound the usual way, an equal distance apart

Hackle: Grey heron, from tail (tied in at the point as usual) wound alongside gold tinsel

Throat: Golden pheasant red breast, two turns

Wings: Two strips of mallard showing brown points and light roots

The feathers of the golden pheasant, especially the crest and tippet feathers, are among the most popular of all fly tying materials.

fly: '…if you angle for him with a flie (which he will rise at like a Trout) the flie must be made of a large hook, which hook must carry six wings, or four at least…'.

Richard Bowlker, in his *Art of Angling*, published in the mid 18th century, had this to say: 'The artificial flies should generally be of large dimensions, and of a gaudy glittering colour; the Dragon Fly, and King's Fisher, are particularly adapted for Salmon fishing… although Salmon will take almost any of the flies used for Trout, if made larger than usual.'

By the early 19th century fly fishing for salmon was a growing sport in Britain, facilitated by advances in rod, reel and line technology, and by a rapidly extending network of improved roads. During this period regional differences in salmon fly patterns were starting to emerge, and in Ireland there was a growing trend towards 'gaudy glittering colour' through the use of feathers from exotic birds, a trend that was later to have a huge impact in Scotland and England (see page 60 [Silver Doctor]). In Scotland, however, where recognisable fly tying styles were being developed on specific salmon rivers – especially the Spey and the Dee – the flies in the first decades of the 19th century were generally much more sober.

TWEED AND DEE

Given their relative isolation, it isn't surprising that the various salmon rivers of Scotland developed their own styles of fly, nor that the flies were tied using largely local materials. It is fortunate for us that the excellent fishing and the aristocratic landowners attracted anglers with time on their hands to enjoy the hospitality and record some of the fly patterns.

William Scrope, writing in 1843 (*Days and Nights of Salmon-fishing in the Tweed*) records the tying instructions for Tweed flies with such intriguing names as Meg in Her Braws and Kinmont Willie, and in his *Angler's Companion to the Rivers and Lochs of Scotland*, published in 1847, Thomas Stoddart includes an illustration of six Tweed flies in use at the time.

Examples of the long and slender strip-winged flies of the River Dee, such as the Balmoral, the Dunt and the Akroyd, are described in some detail by Kelson, who was to play a major role in the popularity of the fully dressed salmon fly. Many of the Dee flies had long, flowing heron hackles, a feature that they shared with the flies from the Spey valley.

STRATHSPEY

Our record of the traditional Spey flies is even better, thanks largely to the efforts of Arthur Edward Knox, a personal friend of Charles Gordon-Lennox, Duke of Richmond and Gordon, and a frequent visitor to the Duke's Speyside estate. In *Autumns on the Spey* (1872), Knox gives detailed descriptions of what were already being termed 'old Spey flies'. Sadly, not one of them is illustrated, but we can be confident that the descriptions are accurate as Knox himself was an accomplished ornithologist and his source for the flies was none other than Geordie Shanks, head ghillie at Gordon Castle for more than 50 years and a man who, it is said, knew more about the river, the fish and the fly fishing than anyone else.

TWEED FLIES.

Reeve lith.

Stoddart includes an illustration of six Tweed flies, all of which have mohair bodies, tail tufts of yellow or orange feather fibres, and wings of mallard, teal, turkey or pheasant feathers.

Discovered Treasure

In 2008, John Shewey travelled to Speyside to carry out research. Having tracked down Geordie Shanks's former home in the village of Craigellachie, he visited the nearby Craigellachie Hotel and was able to identify a collection of Spey flies on the hotel wall as having been tied by Geordie himself, which no-one had realised. The hotel allowed the priceless collection to be shipped to the USA so that John could photograph and study them.

The Craigellachie Hotel stands close to the River Spey in the village in which Geordie Shanks was born and spent his life. Craigellachie lies at the confluence of the Spey and Fiddich rivers, in the heart of Scotch whisky country.

LADY CAROLINE GORDON

The Spey flies, tied on long shanked hooks, were generally dubbed with Berlin wool, had a flowing body hackle of rooster tail or saddle, or of heron hackle, with a counter-wrapped gold or silver rib, and had distinctive wings of bronze mallard strips tied low and tent-like, curving over the body like an upturned boat hull.

The fly known as Lady Caroline is a classic example of the Spey fly, and yet it does not appear in Knox's list of 16. Nonetheless there is every reason to suppose that it was created by Geordie Shanks. John Shewey of Oregon, author of *Spey Flies and Dee Flies: Their History and Construction (2002)* and an expert on the subject, makes a convincing argument that Shanks, with his long connection to the Gordon family, designed the fly after Knox had compiled his list and named it after the young Lady Caroline Elizabeth Gordon-Lennox, daughter of the Duke of Richmond and Gordon, then in her late twenties. Several other Spey flies bear the names of family members at that time, and it is thought that they were all the work of Geordie Shanks. According to Kelson, Shanks was also the originator of the Miss Grant, the only Spey fly other than the Lady Caroline to sport a tail.

THE SPEY TODAY

A few of the traditional Spey flies are still tied and used today, the Lady Caroline – the most famous of all – being a very popular and deadly fly not only for Atlantic salmon but also for steelhead in the Great Lakes and in the Pacific Northwest, where it is also fished for Pacific salmon. The long flowing body hackle and the slim wings give the Spey fly a unique action in the water, creating a very lifelike impression of a shrimp or prawn, significant food items in the diet of the ocean-going salmon.

The Spey fly has also contributed to a new generation of specifically steelhead flies, such as Syd Glasso's Sol Duc Spey (see page 130), and there is a resurgence of interest in this genre along the American Pacific coast.

NEW MATERIALS

The choice of materials for the tyer and have changed in the last 150 years and the reddish brown spey cock hackle that was formerly taken from the sides of the tails of specially bred chickens (now thought to be extinct) is now replaced by schlappen.

The poor heron, which once came under a lot of pressure, particularly in the areas around the Spey and the Dee, is now fully protected and the hackle material that has taken its place, having similar colour and length, comes from blue-eared pheasants bred for the purpose.

Although the feathers of the blue-eared pheasant are less free flowing than those of the heron when the fly is in the water, they have a very similar colour, shape and structure and are a popular choice for Spey fly tyers.

Royal Coachman

YEAR: 1878 **FLY TYER:** John Haily **LOCATION:** New York, USA

The Original Recipe

Hook
Down eye wet fly #10–#16

Thread
Black tying silk

Tail
Golden pheasant
tippet fibres

Body
Peacock herl

Central body
Red tying silk or floss

Throat hackle
Brown hen hackle

Wings
Matching slips of white
duck quill

Head
Varnished black tying silk

This fly is included here partly because it is so visually attractive (both to the angler and, it would seem, the fish) and partly because its history throws light on the kinds of transformations that took place when British flies came to America. It also provides a great opportunity for name dropping.

'If I were asked which fly was the most killing at all times and under all circumstances, I should unhesitatingly say the Coachman. I have tried the Coachman noon and night, in bright and in dark days, in roiled and in clear waters, and it was taken more persistently than any other fly I have ever seen.' **A.C. Heffenger of Portsmouth, NH (c.1890)**

BRITISH FOREBEAR

In its original form the Coachman was created in England in the 1830s by one Tom Bosworth, a keen and accomplished angler and the carriage driver to a succession of British monarchs from King George IV, through William IV to Queen Victoria. The first of these was on the throne when Tom first wound a body of peacock herl, wrapped a brown hackle and tied on two backward-slanting slips of white wing pinion for wings. He intended this wet fly for night fishing but it proved equally effective in the daytime, and Tom later added a grey-winged version called the Leadwing Coachman, using grey mallard slips for wings and looking somewhat like a grey caddisfly. Both these flies made their way across the Atlantic, where they became extremely popular – ridiculously so.

The Leadwing Coachman may be taken by fish to represent a freshly emerged grey sedge / caddis fly or a female swimming down through the water column to lay her eggs, which occurs in many caddis species.

Thaddeus Norris swore by both these flies and used pigeon, gull and blue heron feathers to create three successively darker version of the Leadwing Coachman, and Mary Orvis Marbury, the daughter of Charles F. Orvis, writing in 1892, saw fit to say, 'The Coachman is, perhaps, the most general favorite of any fly used in America…'.

Her book, *Favorite Flies and Their Histories*, provides plenty of supporting evidence for her assertion. Her father had sent out a letter several years earlier to anglers throughout the USA and Canada asking for, among other things, a list of their favourite flies. The majority of her book is composed of the anglers' responses – hence the title – and a remarkable number of the American respondents cite the Coachman among their top flies.

A good number of fishers also ranked one of the world's most recognisable flies – the Royal Coachman – among their top choices. This fly was reputedly created in New York City in 1878 by a professional fly-dresser – and possibly the first vendor of fly tying materials in the USA – named John Haily, who had a store on Henry Street. In response to a client's request for some Coachmen that would be extra strong, Haily added a band of red silk in the middle of the fly to protect the peacock herl body and prevent it from fraying. In its original form it lacked the red tag that became part of its final look. In his own words, taken from a letter he wrote to Charles Orvis, 'I have also added a tail of the barred feathers of the wood-duck, and I think it makes a very handsome fly.' Few people would disagree. Within a few years it was to become one of America's most popular flies for brown trout – especially large ones.

Charles and a few friends, including his brother, were examining an example of the fly that Haily had sent when one of them said, 'Here is a fly intended to be a Coachman, yet it is not the true Coachman; it is quite unlike it, and what can you call it?' According to Mary Orvis Marbury, her uncle chimed in, 'Oh, that is easy enough; call it the Royal Coachman, it is so finely dressed!' The regal title – singularly apt given that the inventor of the original fly was indeed a royal coachman – not only stuck but has also been taken up by a host of flies that share the Royal Coachman's sartorial flair.

THE ROYAL LINEAGE

When Theodore Gordon, creator of the Quill Gordon (see page 72), began investigating dry flies in the early 1890s, he designed floating versions of several common wet flies, and one of these was the Royal Coachman. The upright pinion slip wings were replaced with outward curving white male wood duck breast feathers and the fly became the Fan Wing Royal Coachman in his hands. He was a professional fly tyer and at the request of Leslie Petrie he also created a version using yellow silk in place of the red – the Petrie Royal.

Edward R. Hewitt applied his bi-visible technique (see page 21) to the Royal Coachman by doing away with the wings and adding a white hackle

The bright plumage of the wood duck was once highly prized by European hat makers, but it is the subtle beauty of the flank feathers that is attractive to fly tyers.

in front of the standard brown hackle, and the Royal Coachman Bi-visible soon proved its worth on the Neversink.

Over the years the barred wood duck feather tail has generally given way to golden pheasant tippet for most Royal patterns, but red and brown hackle, deer, moose, and elk hair have also been used. Variations on the theme include a soft-hackled Royal Coachman, a bucktail streamer, a hair-bodied Royal Humpy and the Royal Trude, with a white hair down-wing, that can be used dry or wet.

Its creator was Carter Harrison from Chicago, who tied it at A.S. Trude's Idaho ranch near Henry's Fork in 1906. The first version was a joke, tied on a gaff hook using red yarn from a rug and hair from the family's spaniel, that Carter presented to his host, but in the sober light of day he tied the design for real and tried it out on the Buffalo River, where the cutthroat trout gave it their seal of approval.

THE ROYAL WULFF

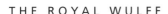

One of the Royal Coachman's most distinguished descendants is a highly buoyant hair-wing version with a split or single wing of white calf tail, invented by Q.L. Quackenbush in about 1930 for use in the Catskills and first tied by Reuben Cross (initially with an impala tail wing). Quackenbush's fellow members in the Beaverkill Trout Club called it the Quack Royal but, due to its similarity to the Lee Wulff hair-wing patterns (see page 108) that had been developed just a year or two earlier in the Adirondacks to the north, it soon became known as the Royal Wulff. It remains a very popular fly today.

What the Royal Coachman and its many cousins actually represent to the fish remains a mystery, with suggestions ranging from flying ants to certain mayfly species, but it remains an effective attractor pattern and that shiny red cummerbund continues to work its magic.

Tough, buoyant and highly visible from above and below, the Royal Wulff seems to be attractive to both fish and fishers alike.

'The best trout fly, according to my experience, is the Coachman.' **Dr J.H. Baxter, Washington, DC (c.1890)**

Little Marryat

YEAR: c.1876   **FLY TYER:** George Selwyn Marryat   **LOCATION:** Hampshire, England

The Original Recipe

Hook
Dry fly up-eye #10–#16

Tail
Brown spade hackle fibres

Thread
Dark brown tying silk

Body
Dubbed grey rabbit fur

Wings
Matched natural duck quill slips

Hackle
Two brown dry fly hackles

A fly that resembles various members of the mayfly family, which settles naturally on the water and that floats well, the Little Marryat is a testimony to the vital role played by George Selwyn Marryat in the evolution of dry fly fishing. He was an accomplished angler, a knowledgeable chalk stream entomologist, a meticulous and innovative fly tyer and, most importantly, a tutor and mentor to Frederic Halford, who put it all into print.

CHALK STREAM BRETHREN

Marryat learnt to fish the downstream wet fly on the River Frome in Dorset as a teenager in the 1850s, and had tried the dry fly on the Itchen, one of England's finest chalk streams, while a student at Winchester College. After spending six years in the army and serving in India, George Marryat worked in Australia for several years and then returned to England, finally settling in Hampshire with his new wife in 1874. Now the dry fly was a growing trend on some rivers, including the nearby River Test, and Marryat embraced the possibilities wholeheartedly, soon becoming an extremely proficient dry fly angler – within the technological constraints of the time. Fly design, and the fact that the eyeless hooks were whipped to gut, meant that smaller patterns soon sank beneath the surface. The only flies that would float for longer were the larger patterns. They could only be fished when a suitable hatch, of *E. danica* for example, was taking place, and even they had their limitations. Dry fly fishing required the use of false casting to dry the fly and anglers would commonly 'crack the whip' on the back cast to rid the fly of moisture. This weakened the gut to breaking point. Marryat – who was by now an expert fly tyer – and several of his co-members in the Houghton Fly Fishing Club would soon bring about some essential changes.

With its clear, shallow water, gently waving weed and manicured banks, the River Itchen, which has played such a key role in dry fly history, is the archetypal English chalk stream.

HOOKS AND TIES

Marryat was undoubtedly the right man in the right place at the right time. As one of the lease holders of the famous Abbot's Barton stretch of the River Itchen, he met other like-minded – and single-minded – fly anglers with whom he could discuss every aspect of the art. One of these was

H.S. Hall, who was working to design an effective good quality eyed hook. Eyed hooks were nothing new. They had been around throughout history – and even prehistory – but the quality had always been poor. With the availability of better and more suitable steel in the 19th century there had been several attempts to market mass-produced eyed hooks, but they still hadn't caught on. Now Hall was trying to design a lighter hook with the ideal bend and the right eye.

Marryat in the meantime was intent upon designing a fly that resembled the natural mayfly, that would land realistically on the surface of the water and would be light enough to stay there. He took his research seriously, collecting insects at the riverbank, taking them home and mounting them, or dissecting them and studying them under the microscope. He then put his findings into practice on the fly-tying bench, and developed the 'paired split wing', using matching slips cut from duck quills on opposite sides of the bird. These were tied upright, 'good' sides facing inwards, naturally curving away from each other. To this he added a stiff cock-hackle wound just at the front of the fly, rather than wound along the body. He also tied flies 'double dressed', with each wing composed of two quill slips, and he fished these dry fly patterns in the 1870s.

Like Hall, Marryat was interested in a better hook, and he was more than willing to share his fly-tying findings with Hall. The collaboration between the two men led eventually to the development of the light-wire, up-eyed 'Snecky-Limerick' hook with an offset point and, later on, a bronzed finish. It complemented Marryat's patterns to produce a light and realistic mayfly that landed gently and floated. A reliable knot for tying the fly to the tippet – and one that encouraged the fly to land and remain in an upright 'cocked' position – was provided by another friend of theirs, Major W.G. Turle.

HITTING THE MARKET

Marryat showed Hall how to tie flies in this style, and Hall wrote instructive articles about the new flies in *The Field* (with little mention of Marryat at the time). In the early 1880s, a commercial fly tyer in the northwest of England called George Holland tied some of these patterns on the basis of Hall's articles and sent them to Hall for his approval. This led to

'It was his great characteristic to be careless of himself and thoughtful for others. In every, true sense he was a thorough sportsman and gentleman and as a fly fisher he had no equal. Marryat was more instrumental in bringing the dry fly to its present stage of development than any fisherman that exists.' **Dr. Thomas Sanctuary, The Field (March 1896)**

Holland moving south in 1885 and setting up his business in Salisbury, very close to where Marryat was living by then. Under Marryat's instruction, he tied and sold the split-winged flies, eventually tying them so well that Marryat ceased to tie them himself. By now dry fly fishing was becoming the vogue, and the flies were extremely popular. So were Hall's new hooks, as many other dry fly anglers were searching for a suitable hook on which to tie their flies. Hall's successful design laid the foundation for the modern dry fly hook, and the up-eyed English Mayfly Snecky Limerick hook is still available today.

MARRYAT'S FLIES

George Selwyn Marryat designed and tied many innovative flies, including a number of wet flies (he also enjoyed wet fly angling on the rain-fed rivers of northern and south-western England), but his name is associated with two dry flies – the Quill Marryat and the Little Marryat. He was by no means the first to use it, but both he and Hall, and later Frederic Halford, appreciated the quill body for its lightness on the water and its ability to convey a segmented body. The Little Marryat, on the other hand, has a lightly dubbed body of fur. Both flies are considered good imitations of pale mayflies, and in the USA the name Little Marryat is now commonly applied to mayflies of the *Epeorus* and *Ephemerella* genera.

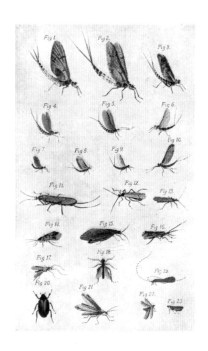

Through his Book on Angling (this illustration of Natural Trout Flies comes from the 1920 edition), and through his role as angling editor of The Field *magazine, Francis Francis exerted considerable influence over the development of fly fishing both in Britain and in North America.*

THE GREAT COLLABORATION

As well as working with Hall and Holland, Marryat shared a great deal of his knowledge with his close friend Francis Francis, angling editor of *The Field* magazine, a fellow lease holder on the Abbot's Barton water and the author of *A Book on Angling*, published in 1867 (before Marryat met him). Although Marryat refrained from writing any articles himself, he undoubtedly influenced Francis's contributions to the magazine, and through them the fly fishing community.

More important still was his partnership with a man whose writings were to define both the practice and the philosophy of dry fly angling for a generation, and whose influence over the sport can still be felt today – Frederic M. Halford (see page 68).

Silver Doctor

YEAR: 1880   **FLY TYER:** James Wright   **LOCATION:** Roxburghshire, Scotland

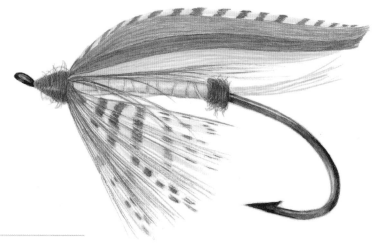

The Original Recipe

Hook
Salmon wet fly, #4–#2/0

Thread
Red tying silk

Tag
Silver wire and yellow silk
or floss (optional)

Tail
Golden pheasant crest

Butt and head
Dubbed red wool

Body
Oval silver tinsel over
flat silver tinsel

Throat hackle
Blue and guinea fowl

Wing
Married feather fibres –
see Kelson's recipe (page 65)

During the first half of the 19th century, while the sombre local Scottish salmon flies were reigning supreme on their respective rivers, the influence of a much more colourful style of fly tying was growing. After 1850 the increasingly complex and gaudy Victorian 'fully dressed' fly, of which the Silver Doctor is a fine example, was to sweep the salmon-fishing world. The style was to hold sway well into the 1900s.

A COLOURFUL HISTORY

For centuries, fly tyers had been adding colour to some of their patterns by using the feathers of exotic birds when they could get them. The English angler and writer Richard Franck, whose *Northern Memoirs* were written in the mid 1600s, recommended that the fly tyer's bag should contain 'feathers from the capon, partridge, peacock, pheasant, mallard, smith, teal, snite, parrot, heronshaw, paraketta, bittern, hobby, phlimingo, or Indian-flush; but the mockaw, without exception, gives flames of life to the hackle.'

Robert Venables, just a few years later, wrote, '...the Salmon flies must be made with wings standing one behind the other, whether two or four; also he delights in the most gaudy and orient colours you can choose...'.

In 1816 George Bainbridge wrote that salmon '...are however so capricious, that they will not unfrequently rise at an extremely gaudy fly, which bears no resemblance to nature, in preference even to a real wasp or Dragon fly...' and added that, 'In the dressing of the gaudy flies for Salmon the maker may exercise his fancy as he pleases, for it is impossible for him to be too extravagant in his ideas'.

Bainbridge's book, *The Fly Fisher's Guide*, was the first to include colour plates of the flies, and his illustration of a 'gaudy fly' shows that even he had no idea what was coming. Admittedly there was red and

'...in this country the Silver Doctor salmon fly [top left] has proved effectual under so many circumstances, and for such a variety of fish, that it is probably valued by American anglers more than any other salmon fly.'
Mary Orvis Marbury,
Favorite Flies and Their Histories **(1892)**

yellow in the pattern, and a wing of black and white guinea fowl feather, but it was positively drab compared with what was just around the corner.

'No. 4. differs materially from those preceding, and is given in order to describe the method of dressing gaudy flies; which, however fanciful or varied in shade or materials, will frequently raise fish when all the imitations of nature have proved unsuccessful: indeed so fastidious and whimsical are the Salmon at times, that the more brilliant and extravagant the fly, the more certain is the Angler of diversion.' **George C. Bainbridge, *The Fly Fisher's Guide* (1816)**

IRISH INFLUENCE

The move towards increased use of colourful feathers in salmon flies appears to have begun in Ireland. Irish flies had commonly featured 'mixed wings' composed of bundles of two, three, or even four different kinds of feather fibres (the wings of Scottish flies, in contrast, were made of a single kind of feather), but from the last decade of the 18th century onwards colourful plumage, which was becoming more readily available, started to replace some of the other sombre tying materials in these Irish mixed wings. After about 1810 these bright and more complex flies, tied to strict patterns, started to show up on the banks of the Scottish rivers.

By the 1840s, salmon fishing in Britain was becoming an increasingly popular sport, driven in part by the expanding railway network that made access to the best salmon waters so much easier. While locals and traditionalists were hesitant and even antagonistic towards the new breed of flies, the new salmon fishers, many of them from the south of England, embraced the exciting new patterns, egged on by fly tyers and suppliers such as William Blacker.

The 1855 edition of William Blacker's Art of Fly Making *included colour plates such as this one showing bright Irish and Scottish flies such as the Ballyshannon, Killarney and McPherson.*

Born in Ireland in 1814, Blacker moved to London in about 1840 where he opened a tackle business. He was also a writer and a remarkable fly tyer, and his book, *Blacker's Art of Fly Making*, was revolutionary. The 1855 edition gave detailed instructions for tying many different kinds of fly, including salmon flies, as well as how to dye the feathers, but also contained actual samples of the requisite feathers and examples of some of the flies themselves.

Blacker even included physical examples, from '1. The hook is tied on the gut' to '6. The wings are turned in their proper place, the head formed, and secured with the tying silk.'

His general instructions on tying Irish and Scottish salmon flies are revealing. To create the wing of the Irish fly, the tyer must mix together fibres from the feathers of 10 species of bird, including the blue macaw, Amazon parrot and orange macaw. For the Scottish fly's wings, 'Clip off from the black and white turkey's tail feather two pieces the eighth of an inch wide...'.

The mixed wing by this time had advanced from being merely a bundle of mixed fibres to being two identical bundles, but an even greater advance was to follow.

FULLY DRESSED FEVER

The second half of the 19th century saw an explosion of creativity in salmon fly design. Toppings – long, bright feather fibres that over-arch the wing – were introduced, as were cheeks of jungle cock nail feathers and, after about 1870, the married wing. Now, rather than simply bundling different fibres together to form a multi-coloured wing, it was found that because the barbs of different feathers will lock or zip together, it is possible to 'marry' different quill segments and create a continuous multi-coloured wing.

In the course of a few decades the selection of available salmon flies rocketed from a few dozen rather restrained patterns to literally hundreds

of rainbow creations, in some cases composed of dozens of individual
feathers, requiring the development of ever more sophisticated tying
techniques. They were – and still are – true works of art. Indeed, some
would, and did, say that these 'fully dressed' flies of the Victorian era had
more to do with art than with catching fish, but they certainly had the
salmon anglers hooked and they kept flying off the shelf.

George Kelson – whose book *The Salmon Fly*, published in 1895,
defines the genre – was both a chronicler and an impresario of this arcane
world. Every element of the fly had a significance that made it suitable
for particular fish in certain waters and conditions. The fish, it was
maintained, soon became indifferent towards patterns they had seen and
therefore needed new stimuli. Any salmon fisher worthy of
the name had to have the latest fly for the river he was on,
and the demand for these flies, and hence their prices,
soared – for a while.

Kelson's book – which provides tying directions
for more than 300 flies – probably marks the crest of
this wave. By the end of the century the philosophy
of the fully dressed fly was being questioned and
Kelson's position as the salmon fly guru was teetering.
Nonetheless, many of the patterns were undeniably
effective and although the fever may have died down
these flies continued to dominate salmon fishing until
the introduction of the hair wing and a process of
simplification after the First World War.

Kelson's Silver Doctor Recipe

Tag: Silver twist and yellow silk

Tail: A topping (the inventor sometimes adds Chatterer)

Butt: Scarlet wool

Body: Silver tinsel

Ribs: Silver tinsel (oval)

Throat: Blue hackle and Gallina

Wings: Strands of tippet, summer duck, pintail, gold pheasant tail, swan dyed light yellow and light blue, bustard, mallard and a topping

Horns: Blue macaw

Head: Scarlet wool

Keslon's book dealt in fine detail with the tying of some 300 flies, and included colour illustrations of more than 50 of these intricate works of art.

THE SILVER DOCTOR

This fully dressed Victorian fly, with its multi-coloured married wing, is a great example of the genre. Its creator, Scotsman James Wright, was hailed as one of the greatest fly tyers, winning several awards for excellence. The Silver Doctor, one of only a small number of salmon flies with a silver body, became very popular in Norway and Canada, and remains so. Its colour combination has served as the basis for many 20th-century versions, such as hair wings, buck-tail streamers and many feathered adaptations of the original, for everything from salmon and steelhead to pike and bass.

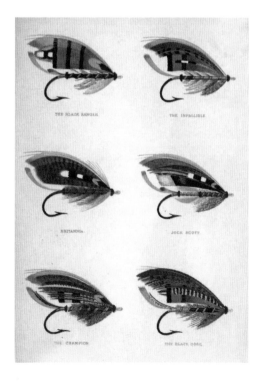

Black Gnat

YEAR: 1885   **FLY TYER:** Frederic Halford   **LOCATION:** Hampshire, England

𝒯𝒽𝑒 **Original Recipe**

Hook
Dry fly hook, #14–#20

Body
Stripped black chaffinch
tail-feather quill

Thread
Black tying silk

Hackle
Cock starling hackle

Wing
Matched slips of pale starling
wing quill

In his book *Floating Flies and How to Dress Them*, published in 1886, Frederic Michael Halford joined a succession of anglers who have tried to create a faithful and effective representation of the black gnat. His version, based on acute attention to detail, is among the most lifelike of the dry patterns. However, it is not for his flies that he is best remembered. Halford's highly acclaimed expositions of the practice of dry fly fishing had an ethical aspect that imbued the sport with an almost religious quality and brought about a schism in the fraternity that still exists today.

FIRST THE FLY

Gnats are members of the *Bibionidae* family within the order Diptera, the 'true' or two-winged flies. The chironomids, or non-biting midges, are members of the same order, but whereas the midges spend the majority of their lives underwater, the gnats – also known as March flies and lovebugs – are purely terrestrial. It's just lucky for the fish and the angler that they breed in moist places and often end up in the water.

In Europe the black gnat is *Bibio johannis*. The larger hawthorn fly and heather fly are closely related, and the Hawthorn and Bibio artificials represent these. There are many members of the family and every continent except Antarctica has its equivalents. As larvae they live underground and after pupating they hatch in their thousands, generally later than the mayflies. The adults mate on vegetation and then take to the air, often with the male still attached to the female but facing backwards in a tail-to-tail position. It's not the ideal way to fly and the post-coital couples stand a good chance of falling into water. Unencumbered females die after depositing their eggs in the ground and then they too fall from the air, as do the spent males. At these times the fish will feast on the dead and dying gnats to the exclusion of all else.

The pale wings of the European black gnat are characteristically folded flat along the top of the abdomen. Gnat patterns can be tied as small as a #22.

Many fly tyers before and since have created black gnat patterns. The features of the natural are its small size, glossy black body, pale/translucent wings and dangling black legs. Charles Cotton gave his a dubbing body of black water-dog or young coot's down with a wing of pale mallard drake, while Bowlker used black ostrich herl for the body, and modern dry patterns use materials such as floss, polypropylene yarn, closed-cell foam and Mylar. There are also 'Knotted Midge' patterns that simulate the male and female joined at the tail using, for example, a black hackle at each end of a long shank hook.

Halford focused on the shiny abdomen and thorax, creating the body from a stripped black chaffinch tail-feather quill that was glossy, light and non-absorbent. Taking account of the fact that wings of the female are longer than those of the male, he gave two versions of the wings, and the cock starling hackle is worked in front of these. The illustrations in *Floating Flies* show the wings set much higher than is seen in the natural, and modern tyers set the wings low over the body.

The title spread of Martin Mosely's Dry-Fly Fisherman's Entomology, *a supplement to Halford's* Dry-Fly Man's Handbook, *depicts 'Detached Badger at Work', using the great man's pen name.*

FATEFUL MEETING

In the spring of 1879, Frederic Halford was invited to fish the famous Abbot's Barton water on the River Itchen. After an uneventful morning he visited the fly shop of John Hammond in nearby Winchester, where he was introduced to another visitor – the celebrated George Selwyn Marryat. Halford was undoubtedly intimidated but he had been collecting and studying aquatic insects for several years and the two men had a great deal to discuss. Marryat must have been impressed at the younger man's knowledge, for he invited Halford to join him, Francis Francis and another friend on the Test a couple of days later. It proved to be the start of a friendship and a 16-year collaboration that changed the course of dry fly fishing.

"Detached Badger at Work."

Halford, who had started his fishing days as a bait angler and had learnt to fish the wet fly on the River Wandle in London, had now been fishing the Test for a couple of years – and he was a committed dry fly man. He was a keen and knowledgeable entomologist and had been studying the aquatic insects of the rivers he had been fishing, as had Marryat, but he soon admitted that he had a lot to learn about fly tying. Marryat was more than happy to teach him all that he knew, and the two of them then continued to work together to study and improve every aspect of dry fly fishing, from fly tying techniques and the behaviour of the natural insects to hooks, knots and casting methods. The fly lines of the time imposed their own limitations on presentation, and Halford and Marryat contacted a manufacturer to work with them and develop a more supple floating line that would cast more easily. In the process they created the prototype of the modern double-tapered line.

Halford's second book, Dry-Fly Fishing in Theory and Practice *(of which this illustration, 'Landing a Trout,' forms the frontispiece), was to prove an even greater success than his first.*

FLOATING FLIES

In 1886 Halford's *Floating Flies* was published. Marryat had declined to be the co-author, but Halford was wholehearted in his acknowledgement of Marryat's contribution, referring to him as 'one of the best, if not the best dry-fly fisherman in England'. The book dealt with dyeing feathers in various colours for particular flies and with the different ways of tying wings and hackles on eyed hooks, as well as providing instructions for tying more than 80 dry flies, many of which are attributed to Marryat.

In his final chapter – Hints to Dry-Fly Fishermen – he gives advice on how to fish the dry fly, but already there are signs of a hidden agenda. After acknowledging that 'it is as well not to enter on any controversy as to the comparative merits of the two schools of fly-fishing: the wet or North Country style, and the dry or South Country style', he goes on to say that 'Each is beyond doubt effective in its own particular streams…'. Dry fly and wet fly fishing are already diverging into two camps, and Halford is suggesting that the southern chalk streams are the domain of the dry fly angler. This was to become a bone of contention.

'Now, there are two ways of fly-fishing, viz. with the dry fly and with the wet fly. Some fishermen always use one plan, others almost as pertinaciously use the other. To use either of them invariably is wrong.' **Francis Francis, *A Book on Angling* (1867)**

A little later in the chapter Halford offers the reader a definition of dry fly fishing, one that is worth quoting in full as it was to become the catechism of the dry fly faithful.

'To define dry-fly fishing, I should describe it as presenting to the rising fish the best possible imitation of the insect on which he is feeding, in its natural position. To analyze this further, it is necessary, firstly, to find a fish feeding on the winged insect; secondly, to present to him a good imitation of this insect, both as to size and colour; thirdly, to present it to him in its natural position, or floating on the surface of the water with its wings up, or what we technically term "cocked"; fourthly, to put the fly lightly on the water, so that it floats accurately over him without drag; and fifthly, to take care that all these conditions have been fulfilled before the fish has seen the angler or the reflection of his rod.'

> 'The reason that all other kinds of fishermen look up to the dry-fly purist is not that he catches more fish than they; on the contrary, it is because he catches fewer. His is the sport in its purest, most impractical, least material form.' **William Humphrey, *My Moby Dick* (1978)**

This isn't just a statement of what the dry fly angler does: it is what the dry fly angler should do. The quarry is the rising fish. If there are no rising fish, there is no fishing. If the fish appear to be rising but there are no winged insects visible then they are taking food items just beneath the surface and the dry fly angler should not cast, even though, as Halford admits, the fish 'may be tempted by a fly floating over him'.

STRENGTHENING THE CASE

Halford's book fully lived up to the 'and practice' part of its title, comprising advice on every aspect of fishing the dry fly. This illustration instructs the angler on where to cast on a river.

Halford's next book, *Dry-Fly Fishing in Theory and Practice*, was published in 1889. It was a 345-page masterpiece that, despite being dedicated to his good friend from 'your grateful pupil', was clearly Halford's own work and revealed the full depth of his considerable knowledge of the subject. Sadly, the third edition was to contain an 'In Memoriam' for George Selwyn Marryat, who had died of a stroke on February 14, 1896, at his home in Salisbury at the age of 56.

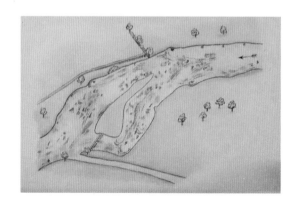

The book was an even greater success than his first, and justifiably so, for it was a complete and thorough practical manual of dry fly fishing. However, on the theory side there was a further hardening of Halford's attitude. While superficially acknowledging the equality of the wet and the dry fly and the skills required to fish them, he nonetheless criticized subsurface fishing, saying that, whereas the dry fly angler is 'fishing the rise,' the wet fly angler can't know where the fish is and is therefore 'fishing the water'. The implication is that this spoils the water for the more discriminating dry fly fisher, and Halford is building a case for 'dry fly only' waters, saying that chalk streams are 'streams in which the dry fly is under all circumstances likely to be more successful than the wet...'.

In *Dry-Fly Fishing* he also strengthened his dictum to the dry fly community itself, writing, 'The purists among dry-fly fishermen will not under any circumstances cast except over rising fish, and prefer to remain idle the entire day rather than attempt to persuade the wary inhabitants of the stream to rise at an artificial fly, unless they have previously seen a natural one taken in the same position.'

THE HALFORDIAN SCHOOL

Over the succeeding years, up until his death in 1914, Halford continued to espouse his increasingly dogmatic dry fly doctrine, and a remarkably large proportion of the fly fishing community, persuaded by the excellence of Halford's highly informative writing and the eloquence of his argument, was carried along on this wave of moral superiority. There were, however, dissenting voices, one among them being an equally talented angler (which Halford certainly was) and an equally eloquent advocate of the subsurface fly by the name of G.E.M. Skues (see page 90).

This photograph, entitled 'Horizontal Cast – Forward Position', forms part of a step-by-step sequence in a very detailed chapter in Dry-Fly Fishing *explaining the different casting styles.*

Halford's writings, including later books such as *Dry Fly Entomology* (1897), *Modern Development of the Dry Fly* (1910) and *The Dry Fly Man's Handbook* (1913), introduced both the methods and the ethics of the English chalk stream dry fly angler to a broad audience, including Theodore Gordon, who began the process of adapting Halford's teachings to the American situation.

Quill Gordon

YEAR: 1892   **FLY TYER:** Theodore Gordon   **LOCATION:** Catskills, New York State, USA

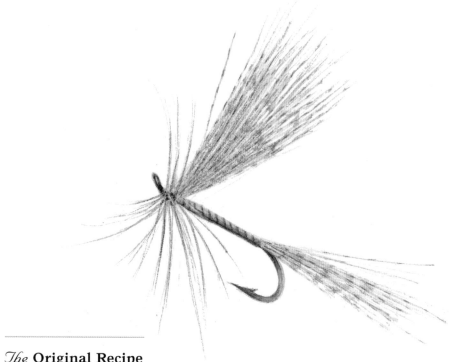

The Original Recipe

Hook
Dry fly up-eye hook, #12–#18

Thread
Cream tying silk

Tail
Medium blue dun fibres

Body
Stripped peacock quill

Wing
Wood duck or dyed mallard flank

Hackle
Medium blue dun

The delicate Quill Gordon has fairly been described as one of the first truly American dry flies, and if Thaddeus Norris was the father of American fly fishing then his disciple, Theodore Gordon, could be – and has been – called the father of dry fly angling in the USA. Gordon's creation marks the start of the Catskill school of fly tying, and it soon made its way across the Atlantic to have an impact on the English dry fly scene, too.

FROM WET TO DRY

Gordon first discovered the joys of fly fishing through the writings of Thaddeus Norris, to whom he referred affectionately as 'Uncle Thad', and it was from Norris's *The American Angler's Book*, published in 1864, that Gordon learnt to tie flies. Although Norris made references to dry flies in his book, American fly fishing at this time was almost exclusively with wet flies, and these were the flies that Gordon tied and fished in the late 1880s.

A decade earlier, in response to the gradual decline in the brook trout population in the eastern United States because of pressure from over-fishing and habitat changes, brown trout had been introduced to eastern streams from Europe. They were now becoming established but were proving perplexingly difficult to catch, responding very differently from the native brook trout and rainbows, harder to tempt with the popular wet

The brook trout (actually a char, a member of the genus Salvelinus) was already under pressure from habitat destruction in Gordon's time and has since disappeared from many water courses.

Due to its association with Theodore Gordon and his efforts to match artificial flies to the local naturals, the Neversink River (seen here at the confluence of the West and East branches) is regarded as the birthplace of American dry fly fishing.

flies of the time but seemingly more willing to take a fly on the surface. Gordon, aware that when a hatch was in progress a wet fly cast upstream stood its best chance of being taken while it was still floating, became intrigued with dry flies and the work of Frederick Halford, and in 1890 he wrote to the great man asking for advice on which patterns might work. In response Halford generously sent Gordon a selection of 48 dry flies that he himself used on the chalk streams of southern England. (This collection, which was to change fundamentally the course of fly fishing in the USA, is now housed at the Catskill Fly Fishing Center and Museum in Livingston Manor, NY.)

FROM EAST TO WEST

Gordon, of course, soon tried them out on his beloved Catskill streams, but therein, as they say, lies the rub. Well, two rubs to be accurate. In the first place, European aquatic insect life is significantly different from that of North America and many of Halford's patterns represented particular European mayfly species. Wet flies had already undergone transformations since their arrival in the USA, and Gordon now found that Halford's English dry flies simply didn't match the hatch.

In the second place, chalk stream flies had been developed for use on relatively smooth, steadily flowing water, settling into the surface film but staying afloat. Transplanted into the rougher, tumbling waters of the Catskill freestone streams, they soon became waterlogged. So it was that Gordon, a completely self-taught fly tyer, set himself the task of designing and tying a much lighter, more buoyant and geographically appropriate fly.

He soon came to the conclusion that 'by following the colors of our own natural flies, which were on the water, I caught more trout, even when the work was rougher and less perfect to the eye.'

His experiments with colours, proportions and materials eventually led him to create a fly that came to define a regional fly tying style, one that is still very much alive and kicking more than a century later.

'We are so tied down to the pursuit of the essential dollar that we lose the best and most innocent pleasures that this old earth affords. Time flies so fast after youth is past that we cannot accomplish one-half the many things we have in mind, or indeed one-half our duties. The only safe and sensible plan is to make other things give way to the essentials, and the first of these is flyfishing.'
John McDonald, *The Complete Fly Fisherman: The Notes and Letters of Theodore Gordon* (1847)

The use of stripped quill for the body was not a new idea. Halford himself was in favour of quill patterns and wrote in his *Floating Flies and How to Dress Them*, with which Gordon was familiar, 'Quill being at the present time the most suitable material, its use is recommended wherever practicable. The quill generally used is a strand from a peacock-eye or end of the tail feather…'. Halford refers to the red quill fly, tied with dyed stripped peacock quill, as 'one of the sheet anchors of a dry-fly fisherman on a strange river'.

Gordon was clearly paying attention, and when it came to formulating his lightweight fly, a stripped natural peacock quill body was his choice. With wings of wood duck flank-feather fibres, a medium blue dun hackle and a tail of hackle fibres, he created a high-riding and buoyant imitation of the mayfly species *Epeorus pleuralis*, one of the earliest hatches in the Catskills. Both the natural and the artificial fly are now best known as the Quill Gordon.

Although he never wrote a book, Gordon was a prolific writer of articles for both British and American magazines such as *The Fishing Gazette* and *Forest and Stream*, and through his writings he passed on his passion for dry fly fishing and his extensive knowledge of the fish and insects of the region that he made his home. His 'tiptoe' style of fly, with its light, upright wings, long tail and long, full hackle, became the template for what has become the Catskill school of fly tying, recognisable world wide.

Gordon's Life

Theodore Gordon was born in Pittsburgh in 1854 into a wealthy New York family, but his father died when he was just four months old and he spent much of his childhood living with relatives in Pennsylvania, where he bait-fished the local limestone creeks. After the end of the Civil War he and his mother moved to Savannah, Georgia, where he found work as a book-keeper, but he was plagued by ill health and after ten years the two of them moved north to New Jersey, where he continued to work in the financial sector. By now he had discovered the writings of Thaddeus Norris, as well as those of several English angling writers, and certainly by 1890 he was a convinced fly fisher. Unenthusiastic about his job, he spent as much time as he could fishing, visiting the Catskills whenever possible, and in 1900 he quit work and moved north to Haversham to live with relatives on his father's side. Five years later he moved again, this time to lodgings beside the Neversink, where he spent the next ten years as a semi-recluse, fishing, writing articles for angling magazines and tying flies for a living. He died, virtually penniless, of tuberculosis in 1915, but left a legacy that continues to influence American fly fishing to this day.

Mickey Finn

YEAR: 1890s **FLY TYER:** Charles Langevin **LOCATION:** Quebec, Canada

The Original Recipe

Hook
4XL streamer hook, #1/0–#8

Body
Flat silver tinsel

Thread
Black tying thread

Wing
Yellow, red, yellow bucktail

Rib
Medium oval tinsel

Head
Varnished black tying thread

The historical use of hair of various kinds in the tying of artificial lures is less well recorded than the use of feathers, but hairwing streamers – usually made from bucktail – were certainly well established in the USA by the middle of the 19th century, and in a form very little different from modern versions. By the end of the century Orvis of Vermont were selling bucktail streamers tied on longshank hooks.

The highly recognisable Mickey Finn was invented in the 1890s and, after several changes of identity, it remains a highly effective fly today for a wide range of predatory fish species.

CANADIAN ORIGINS

The story goes that the creator of this simple bait-fish look alike, with its flash of silver, yellow body and red lateral line, was one Charles Langevin of Quebec. Locally it was called the Langevin, but it didn't become very widely known for several decades. In 1932 the American writer and outdoorsman John Alden Knight was given a 'Red and Yellow Bucktail' by a friend while trout fishing in New York State and it proved to be the only catching fly of the day. (John Alden Knight, incidentally, was the creator of the Solunar tables, which use the relative positions of the Earth, sun and moon to predict the most productive times for hunting and fishing.) In 1936 he caught 75 brook trout on this one pattern, prompting him to give it the name of Assassin, but the name didn't last long. Shortly afterwards Greg Clarke (a keen hunter and angler, a journalist with the *Toronto Star* and a friend and colleague of Ernest Hemingway) rechristened the fly Mickey Finn after reading in *Esquire* magazine that the death of heart-throb Rudolf Valentino ten years earlier was the result of being plied with spiked drinks, or Mickey Finns, by envious bartenders in New York and Hollywood.

The long hair from the tail of the blacktail deer (above), the mule deer and, most commonly, the whitetail deer has been used in North America since the mid 1800s to tie a huge range of 'bucktail' streamers.

Mickey Finns and bucktail streamers in general are popular flies for striped bass on the Atlantic coasts of the USA and Canada, tied on stainless steel hooks in sizes #2/0 to #4/0.

HITTING THE BIG TIME

In 1937 Knight wrote an article about the fly in *Hunting and Fishing* that fired the popular imagination. Its publication coincided with the Sportsmen's Show in New York, and it was estimated that as many as half a million Mickey Finns were tied and sold during the show. The manufacturers, the Weber Lifelike Fly Company of Wisconsin, who had advertised the fly in the same magazine, were overwhelmed by orders for Mickey Finns from across the country.

The colour combination seems to be a winning one, and the sinuous motion of the long bucktail fibres gives life to what is essentially a very simple pattern. Originally tied as a trout fly (and especially effective for cutthroat), the Mickey Finn in a range of sizes is a proven winner in rivers, lakes and oceans around the world for a host of different species, taking large- and smallmouth bass, salmon, steelhead, sea trout, pike, pickerel, garfish and striped bass.

VARIATIONS

Although no-one can say precisely what the Mickey Finn is meant to represent, the red and yellow have given rise to a wide range of variations in different styles and materials, including the marabou Mickey Finn, the Mickey Finn Woolly Bugger, and a feather Mickey Finn in the style of Carrie Stevens (see Gray Ghost, page 106).

The Mickey Finn is also part of a vast family of more naturalistic bucktail streamers that are generally tied with a darker upper half and lighter lower half, and many of them also incorporate a conspicuous

Art Flick's Black-nose Dace bucktail was first tied in the 1940s, and the tinsel body of the original is now often replaced with Mylar tubing.

The colour scheme of the Black-Nose Dace is common to many species of minnow and darter, as well as the juveniles of many freshwater fish that feed upon them.

stripe along the lateral line. This imitates a good many prey species such as minnows, darters and juvenile bass. A good example is the Black-Nose Dace, created by Art Flick, which has a brown upper half, a black stripe, a white belly and a short tuft of red yarn for a tail.

FISHING TECHNIQUES

Streamer fishing for trout on open still waters needs a little speed if the fly is to behave like a fleeing prey fish, and streamers were commonly trolled behind rowing boats in the early days of their use. It is no coincidence that the popularity of this fly pattern saw a rapid growth in the 1920s, when reliable and relatively affordable outboard motors became available. Trolling is still a common streamer technique, giving rise to the accusation that bucktails are not really flies.

In the Pacific Northwest, 'salmon bucktails' made with tail hair from the local blacktail deer were being cast to returning salmon in the river estuaries in the early decades of the 20th century, and now 'bucktailing'

Tied by Bob Hetzler, the two-tone Pearl Mickey, with its pearlescent strands, epoxy head and large eyes, is a Pacific Northwest variation on the original.

for salmon in the ocean has becoming a sport in its own right. For ocean fishing the flies are tied on stainless steel long-shank hooks, sometimes with trailer hooks and with additional bucktail tied on half-way down the shank to increase the length.

Coho salmon, in particular, respond to a bucktail being ripped along the surface and sometimes skipping into the air as the angler swings the rod forward to accelerate the fly.

THE STATE OF THE ART IN 1900

*U*ntil 1800, the story of the development of fly fishing tackle as we know it is largely set in the British Isles, and throughout the first half of the 19th century most of the equipment in use in North America was imported. However, by the middle of the century the United States had adopted, adapted and was steadily improving, especially in the important areas of rods and reels, making advances that would later be taken up on the other side of the Atlantic.

Rods

At the start of the 1800s, rods were still being made from hardwoods such as ash, hickory and hazel, with the relatively recent addition of lancewood and greenheart from abroad, and whole Calcutta cane was making inroads as a material for rod tips. Some rods had male/female joints of wood and brass but the joints

tended to be heavy and unreliable. Rods and joints gradually improved during the first half of the century, but one particular innovation was gaining ground.

While its lightness and strength made cane suitable for rod tips, it was hard to find knot-free lengths, so in the early 1800s makers began splitting the cane and gluing and binding four 'clear' strips together. The resulting rod tip was lighter, stronger and more flexible than whole cane. Hardwood rods with split-cane top sections became common, but it took a while for any maker to consider making the whole rod this way, and by then America had taken the lead.

Samuel Phillipe of Pennsylvania was building entire rods of four-strip split cane in the 1840s, and the first six-strip split Calcutta cane appeared in the 1850s, the first maker being Charles Murphy of New Jersey or Solon

The frontispiece of Mary Orvis Marbury's *Favorite Flies and Their Histories* shows William Cowper Prime and William F. Bridge outside a fishing cabin in the late 1870s. By this time the light and slender split cane rod was rapidly gaining favour.

Phillipe, the son of Samuel. Other manufacturers followed suit, and eventually everyone came round to the hexagonal profile. At that time each rod section was being hand planed and sanded, tested and corrected, to produce the required power and degree of flexion in the final rod, a very time-consuming process with unpredictable results. The next major step forward was the creation by H.L. Leonard of a planing/bevelling machine to produce a consistent and carefully calculated compound taper on every rod. Leonard's rods were quite simply the best at the time – he produced some 200 rods in 1876 – and he literally kept the machine, the heart of his enormously successful business, under lock and key. Others eventually developed similar machines but they had to work out for themselves the secret of his winning taper and it also took a while to discover that Leonard was using a much better kind of cane – Tonkin cane from China.

Salmon rods, up to 17ft (5m) long but now made of greenheart, were no longer spliced but had lighter and more effective ferrules, while trout rods became transformed into shorter, two-piece rods that became all the vogue. This change was strongly influenced by two events in Britain – W.C. Stewart's exhortation to use a short, stiff, single-handed rod and to use the false cast to dry the line and the fly, and the move to dry fly fishing championed by such characters as Halford. Leonard's rods soon found themselves in the hands of the British chalk stream anglers, including G.E.M. Skues, who was fulsome in his praise of the new 'weapon'.

'I think the chief part of the ecstasy of fishing with the fly is to be found in the qualities of the fly rod, and if I am right in this, the more exquisite the rod the keener and more perfect the pleasure to be derived from the sport, a strong argument in favour of perfection in one's weapon for the particular game in hand.' **G.E.M. Skues, *The Flyfishers' Journal*, 1917**

Throughout the 19th century and even into the 20th it was common to have a hardwood butt and middle rod section with a split-cane tip. Ferrule design varied considerably.

Reels

In the course of the 19th century a range of manufacturers, responding to the growing popularity of the sport, put some serious effort into reel design, both in Britain and, to an even greater degree, in the USA. The ineffective British multiplier – primarily used for bait casting – was greatly improved by George Snyder and other precision engineers in Kentucky from 1820 onwards, and larger versions for trolling were developed in New York State, but the quality and design of fly reels, too, moved forward in leaps and bounds.

Fly reels became narrower between the face plates and the diameter of the spools increased to increase the speed of line retrieval, new materials such as aluminium were used, and the old threaded spike fittings gave way first to clamp fittings and then to the plate foot of the modern reel. Rod design incorporated the reel seat to accommodate this. Click mechanisms were introduced to prevent overrun.

On both sides of the Atlantic the number of manufacturers escalated, some mass producing cheap brass reels while others, such as the US companies of Julius Vom Hofe, Pfleuger, Orvis, Leonard and Francis Loomis (who developed an automatic reel) focused on craftsmanship and high quality materials including German silver and hard rubber.

These three reels, all with foot mountings, show the variations in style in the second half of the 19th century.

The J.C. Conroy & Co. reel (c. 1871) is made of German silver, the C.F. Orvis plated brass reel (c. 1885), with its lightweight perforated plate that allows the silk line to dry, set the standard for the early 20th century, and the solid Julius Vom Hofe reel (c. 1890) is faced with black rubber.

More than 100 years after it was first created, the Hardy Perfect reel – in a far more refined form – is still in production.

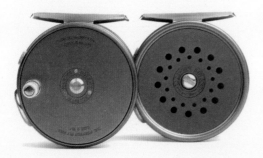

Charles F. Orvis opened his tackle shop in Manchester, Vermont, in 1856 and soon established his company – now the oldest mail-order business in the USA – as an authority on fly fishing tackle.

By the end of the century the leading reel manufacturers in England were Farlow and Co., marketing the Patent Lever Winch (a reel based on a design by George Kelson of salmon fly fame), and Hardy's with their Perfect, which ran on ball-bearings and was easily dismantled for cleaning. The Perfect owed much to the Orvis ventilated narrow spool fly reel, introduced in 1874.

Line

Although plaited and twisted silk lines became available in the early 1800s, they quickly became waterlogged, making them difficult to cast, and they were prone to rotting, so most fly fishers stuck with horsehair until the 1860s and beyond. Finely plaited silk finally won the day when suitable means of dressing it so that it was rot proof and water resistant were developed. Besides, the new rods and reels made it possible for anglers to cast further and to play the fish at greater distances, and only silk could provide the greater lengths of continuous line that were needed. These thinner, lighter lines made even longer casts possible.

As if the silkworm wasn't doing enough to transform fly fishing, another important development that helped to oust horsehair was the introduction of silkworm gut to make 'casts', or leaders, to which the flies could be whipped. Far stronger than horsehair, the raw gut could be drawn through holes of appropriate sizes to create the desired diameter to suit the fly and the quarry, and it also allowed the angler to fish several flies at the same time on droppers. Silkworm gut continued to be used well into the 20th century.

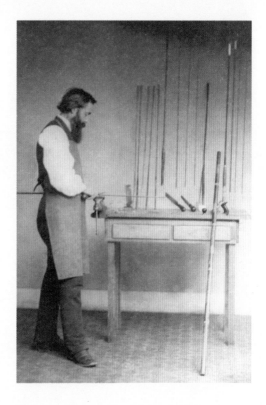

Like several other rodmakers, Hiram L. Leonard was first a gunsmith. His use of a bevelling machine, and his compound taper, were major advances in rod making.

Hooks

The widespread use of gut should have persuaded anglers of the advantages of the eyed hook, since the gut on a whipped fly had a tendency to be brittle when dry and to rot when wet, rendering the fly useless when the gut broke, but throughout most of the 19th century hooks continued to be eyeless. Despite the efforts of several manufacturers, it wasn't until the rise of the dry fly and the introduction of H.S. Hall's hooks in the 1880s that the concept began to gain popularity, and 'blind' hooks were still being manufactured in the 1960s.

Tup's Indispensable

YEAR: 1890   **FLY TYER:** R.S. Austin   **LOCATION:** Tiverton, Devon, England

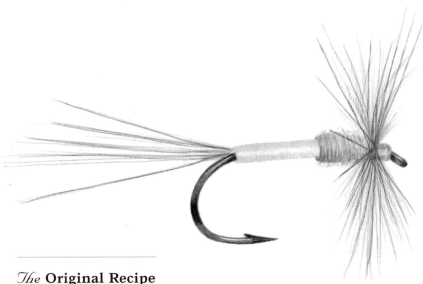

The Original Recipe

Hook:
Dry fly hook, #12–#18

Thorax
Dubbed orange/pink fur mix

Thread
Yellow tying silk

Hackle
Blue dun or honey dun

Tail
Blue dun or honey dun fibres

Head
Varnished yellow tying silk

Abdomen
Yellow tying silk

A relatively simple dry fly with a secret ingredient, Tup's Indispensable, as it became known, was created by a tobacconist in southwest England who, with his daughter Agnes, ran a sideline in fly tying. The fly was greatly admired by G.E.M. Skues, who gave it its name, and by Theodore Gordon, to whom Skues probably sent the fly.

Austin's fly not only became popular on both sides of the Atlantic but it also influenced Skues's thinking on the subject of nymphs.

'The fly on the cast was a Tup's Indispensable, then the latest invention of an ingenious West-Country angler, and, when the red spinner is up, a very killing fly…' **G.E.M. Skues, Minor Tactics of the Chalk Stream (1910)**

A WINNING PATTERN

The exact date on which the fly was first tied is unclear, but it was probably in the early 1890s that R.S. Austin came up with a wingless dry fly pattern that had a tail and hackle of honey dun, and abdomen of yellow silk and a thorax of orangey-pink dubbing composed of cream and red seal's fur, combings from a lemon yellow spaniel – and something else. Austin had considerable success with the fly that he felt was a good imitation of the female spinner of the olive dun and which he himself referred to as a red spinner. In 1900 he sent Skues an example (one on which he had caught several good trout) together with the tying instructions and some of the special dubbing material so that Skues could tie the fly for himself. Skues did so, tried it on the River Itchen and was highly impressed with the re-sults, so impressed that he soon published his findings, naming the fly Tup's Indispensable.

Once fished mainly for salmon, the River Frome in Dorset is now famous for its thriving wild brown trout population. Anglers who have fished its waters include Frederick Halford, George Selwyn Marryat and Roderick Haig-Brown.

The resulting publicity led to the fly quickly becoming very popular, especially in the south-west of Britain, so much so that Skues later wrote that '…Austin became utterly sick of tying it, and one of his customers said that the Dorsetshire Frome [the region's principal chalk stream] stank of Tup's Indispensables from Maiden Newton to the sea'.

Austin insisted on keeping his magic dubbing ingredient a secret from the public but he confided in Skues on condition that he do the same. After Austin's death in 1911 his daughter continued to run the fly tying business and to tie the Indispensable, but when she retired in 1934 she released Skues from his vow of secrecy.

By now Tup's Indispensable was extremely well known and widely respected, and Skues put an end to the conjecture that surrounded the fly by publishing the full details in the *Flyfishers' Club Journal*. The mystery ingredient in the dubbing, it turned out, was hair from the scrotum of a ram, or tup. It was common practice at the time to tie an orange-dyed sponge or cloth to the belly of a ram so that the farmer could see by the presence of dye on a ewe's back whether or not she had been 'tupped'. This dye, possibly aided by a certain amount of urine, gave the tup's scrotal hair a particular hue, and the hair, after being thoroughly washed, apparently

gave Austin's fly that little something that trout found irresistible. It wasn't the fly that was indispensable – it was the part of the tup's anatomy.

This wasn't the first time that the hair of the ram's scrotum had featured in an artificial fly. Writing almost a hundred years earlier, Alexander Mackintosh in his book The Driffield Angler *(from which this is the frontispiece) recommended its use in a green drake pattern, describing the wool as being 'of a beautiful dusty yellow'.*

FISHING IT WET

George Skues, as we shall see, was to play a pivotal role in the development of nymph fishing, and the discoveries that he made while fishing Tup's Indispensable were key. In his book *Minor Tactics of the Chalk Stream*, published in 1910, Skues recounted that for a while after he was first introduced to this fly he fished it only as a dry fly, but on one July day he 'put it over a fish without avail, and cast it a second time without drying it. It was dressed with a soft hackle, and at once went under, and the trout turned at it and missed. Again I cast, and again the trout missed, to fasten soundly at the next offer. It was a discovery for me, and I tried the pattern wet over a number of fish on the same shallow, with most satisfactory results.'

Skues then tried casting the fly to 'bulging fish', trout that were taking food items close to the surface and causing the surface of the water to bulge as they turned, and again the fish found it very attractive.

On the basis of this fly Skues went on to create a small range of nymph patterns but, he wrote, 'for underwater feeders, whether bulging or otherwise, I seldom need anything but Tup's Indispensable, dressed with a very short, soft henny hackle in place of the bright honey or rusty dun used for the floating pattern'.

This soft hackle was to be fundamental to an important line of fly development, not just for Skues but for many others who followed, including James Leisenring and Pete Hidy (who took Tup's Indispensable as the basis for a pattern of their own) and Sylvester Nemes.

The great soft-hackled fly advocate Sylvester Nemes regarded Tup's Indispensable as one of his favourites. This deliberately scruffy version of the fly, with its loose thorax and short hackle, was tied by him.

THE MODERN TUP'S

Over the decades the traditional dry version of this fly has remained a favourite to represent a wide range of mayfly spinners, but there are also parachute versions – with the hackle wound horizontally around an upright and highly visible post – that have the advantage of landing extra softly on the water and offer a silhouette that can resemble an emerger, a dead nymph or a spent spinner.

The materials used for the pink thorax have, unsurprisingly, changed over time, much to the relief of the ram population. Dyed rabbit fur is now a common substitute, sometimes with a little sparkle added, but the Tup's magic seems still to be there.

March Brown

YEAR: 1906   **FLY TYER:** G.E.M. Skues   **LOCATION:** Hampshire, England

The Original Recipe

Hook
Stout wet fly hook, #12–#16

Thread
Crimson tying thread

Tail
Brown or furnace hen hackle fibres

Body
Dubbed hare's mask or hare's ear fur

Rib
Narrow gold tinsel

Hackle
Brown or furnace hen hackle

Wing case
Pheasant tail fibres

While there is no doubt that certain styles of subsurface fly –
North Country spiders among them – have often been taken by
fish as nymphs of various kinds, George Edward MacKenzie Skues
set out deliberately to imitate this stage in the life of aquatic
insects and to develop the necessary techniques to fish them
effectively on the hallowed chalk streams of southern England.
In doing so he founded an entirely new branch of fly fishing and
confronted Frederic Halford and the dry fly school head on.

THE LIGHT DAWNS

In the 1880s and 1890s, fishing in Hampshire meant dry fly fishing, and
so it was for Skues, but over the years several observations led him to
reconsider the merits of the wet fly. In the late 1880s he caught a trout
whose mouth was full of small green insects, which – being no entomologist
at the time – he only later discovered were nymphs. In 1891 he had a
chance encounter on the river bank with none other than Halford himself,
and Skues was quite underwhelmed by the experience. Halford insisted on
telling Skues which fly he should be using but
Skues stuck to his guns and soundly outfished
the great man. The experience gave Skues the
courage to question the accepted wisdom of
the time and the confidence to rely on his own
judgement when he later found that wet
versions of dry flies were very effective under
the water when there were 'bulging' rises and no
insects on the surface. He later admitted that,
given the evidence in front of him, it took him a
remarkably long time to reach the inevitable
conclusion that prior to a hatch the trout were
cruising up and down and taking pre-emergent
nymphs in the surface layers.

The march brown
(Rhithrogena germanica)
is probably the best known
mayfly among British fly
fishers. It hatches early in
the year, and has been copied
by anglers since the time
of Dame Juliana. The
American march brown
(Rhithrogena morrisoni)
is very similar.

When he began to develop his own methods of angling and fly tying, Skues was able to draw on the wealth of wet fly history that had apparently been abandoned in the course of the dry fly love affair, and he went back to writers and practitioners such as Stewart and the North Country school, agreeing with them wholeheartedly that soft hackles imparted life to the fly in the water. Skues was painstaking in his research. He studied the various different kinds of rise exhibited by the fish, he carried out autopsies to determine precisely what the trout were eating, and he used a specially designed net to take samples of insect life from the river, which he was able to use to predict the onset of a hatch. (G.E.M. Skues was the first person to use a marrow spoon to investigate the contents of the trout's stomach without having to kill it.)

George Edward MacKenzie Skues

G.E.M. Skues was born in Newfoundland in 1858 and arrived in England at the age of three. Like Marryat, he attended Winchester College and, also like Marryat, he learnt to fly fish on the nearby River Itchen, catching his first trout when he was 16. At the age of 20 he began a career in law in London, a career that was to last 60 years. Skues never married and throughout his working life he devoted all his spare time to the various aspects of fishing, regularly taking the train down to Winchester to fish his beloved rivers and tying experimental flies during the journey using a hand-held vice. He has been hailed as one of the greatest fly

fishers, and he studied the subsurface world of fish and their food items in every bit as much detail as Halford had studied the surface. He was a prolific writer, penning articles for *The Field* magazine and having four books published. His writings – informative, fascinating and frequently witty – laid the foundation for nymph anglers everywhere and are still well worth reading.

G.E.M. Skues was still fishing at the age of 87, and he has been hailed as one of the greatest anglers as well as an expert in entomology, fly tying and fly fishing tactics.

Ever the diplomat, he couched his method in the same terms as the dry fly anglers, casting the fly upstream to feeding fish, presenting it to the fish in the same way as the natural. The 'only' difference was that these were the nymphal forms below the surface and about to hatch.

In articles for *The Field* magazine, written under the pen name Seaforth and Soforth, Skues put forward his ideas, his discoveries, his methods and his arguments for the importance of subsurface fishing. Halford was also writing articles in the same magazine, with the by-line Detached Badger, and there was a degree of to and fro between them, but there seems to have been very little personal animosity.

Strangely, Halford himself had taken a great interest in nymphs at one time, and both he and Marryat had experimented with fishing nymph patterns. Halford had rejected these types of fly, claiming not only that they were a breach of the dry fly code of ethics and should therefore never be used on a chalk stream, but also that only a small proportion of the fish that took the nymph were successfully hooked and that therefore the method made the fish 'shy and unapproachable'. (In those days a fish landed was a fish heading for the dining table.)

Ironically, Frederic Halford made an exhaustive study of the underwater portion of the green drake's life cycle, and included detailed drawings of the stags of the nymph in his Dry Fly Fishing.

THE GLOVES COME OFF

In 1910, G.E.M. Skues' first book, *Minor Tactics of the Chalk Stream*, was published. Even the title was a shot across the bows of the dry fly school, for Skues was about to prove that nymph fishing was no 'minor tactic'. Much of the book is clearly written, often tongue in cheek, with Halford's criticisms in mind:

'Mr. F. M. Halford, with every desire to be absolutely fair, has, I think, in Chapter II. of *Dry-Fly Fishing in Theory and Practice*, done more than any other man to discredit the wet fly on chalk streams, by the implications, first, that the principle of the dry-fly method – viz., the casting of the fly to a feeding fish in position – is not applicable to the wet-fly method, and, secondly, that on the stillest days, with the hottest sun and the clearest water, the wet fly is utterly hopeless. On both these points I respectfully join issue with him.'

As one might expect from an accomplished lawyer for whom language was his stock in trade, he put forward his arguments brilliantly, basing them on solid scientific observations. He not only showed that the vast majority of the trout's diet is made up of subsurface items (a fact that Halford not only acknowledged but was one of the first to point out) but he demonstrated when and how and with what patterns the fish could be fooled into taking the artificial nymph. He contended the reason Halford and others failed to hook fish properly was that a trout taking the fly beneath the surface was much harder to detect than the blindingly obvious taking of a dry fly on the surface

THE FINAL VOLLEY

In his The Way of a Trout with a Fly, *G.E.M. Skues offer two methods of tying a nymph, saying, 'Representation or suggestion rather than imitation is what the dresser of nymphs should aim at. That is one reason why dubbings outclass quills for bodies of nymphs.'*

In *The Dry-Fly Man's Handbook*, published in 1913, three years after *Minor Tactics*, Halford disputed that nymph anglers were ever actually successful in casting upstream to a feeding fish, and even went so far as to imply that sunk fly anglers were actually snagging fish rather than hooking them legitimately, repeating his accusation that fishing the nymph pricked and scared the fish. At the same time he was prepared to admit that fishing the sunk fly did take skill, so there was an inherent contradiction in his attitude, rooted in his desire to protect the chalk streams as the domain of his chosen style of fishing. Halford died the following year, leaving behind a continuing discussion between the two opposing camps.

Skues' second book, *The Way of a Trout with the Fly* (1921), is considered one of the greatest works on nymph fishing. He continued to refute Halford's position (and even had the temerity to suggest that Halford's spinner patterns verged on being wet flies and that in any case they fished more successfully when sunk), but he also introduced some of the key concepts in nymph fishing.

Among these was the concept of 'kick', which Skues described as 'a quality which every hackled wet fly, for use in rough water, should invariably have. Without it, it is a dead thing; with it, it is alive and struggling; and the fly which is alive and struggling has a fascination for the trout which no dead thing has. How is this quality to be attained ? It is a very simple matter. Finish behind the hackle.' Although subsequent fly tyers have developed other ways of achieving this lifelike movement, kick remains a central concept in the design of soft hackle nymphs.

Throughout the first three decades of the 20th century large stretches of the southern English chalk streams remained exclusively the province of the dry fly. There was a growing number of prominent and eloquent supporters of nymph fishing, but the Halfordian school were entrenched.

The argument over the efficacy and, more importantly, the ethics of the sunk fly method reached a crescendo in February of 1938 when the 'Nymph Debate' was held at the Flyfishers' Club in London. It is difficult now to believe how seriously the angling protagonists took themselves and their preferences given the events that were about to unfold on the world stage. Skues was there to make his case, largely by attacking the doctrine of the late Halford, but the dry fly proponents won the day. Nonetheless, Skues' influence was here to stay and it was already being felt in the USA, where further advances would soon be made.

Slow Learners

Skues commented on the fact that the poorly educated Scottish fly angler John Younger, in his 1839 book *River Angling for Salmon and Trout*, had clearly understood the importance of nymphs when he observed, 'As the trout are feeding on these insects in all states, both at the bottom and as they ascend to the surface, no wonder that people sometimes catch a few trouts with very ill-formed flies, even without wings altogether.' Even he, however, ignored the opportunity that this presented for the fly fisher, continuing, 'Yet this is not a sufficient reason why you should not have a fly formed to give as much as possible the shape, colour, and appearance of the natural fly in its state of fullest perfection…'.

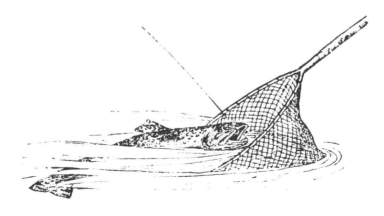

Gold-Ribbed Hare's Ear Nymph

YEAR: c.1910   **FLY TYER:** Anon.   **LOCATION:** England

The Original Recipe

Hook
Nymph hook, #10–#16

Rib
Fine gold wire

Thread
Brown tying thread

Wing case
Pheasant or turkey tail fibres

Tail
Hare's ear guard hairs or
hen feather fibres

Head
Varnished brown tying thread

Body
Hare's ear dubbing

When it comes to all-purpose nymphs, the fly to be found in more fly boxes around the world than any other (with the possible exception of the Pheasant-Tail Nymph) is the Gold-Ribbed Hare's Ear Nymph, or GRHE. It owes its universality to a generalised nymph shape and the special qualities of hare's ear dubbing, a mixture of soft fur and stiff guard hairs that together create a fly that doesn't look exactly like anything but that gives an impression of a great many things, and that's a good enough reason always to carry several.

WET FLY ORIGINS

The material – originally taken from just the ear of the hare but later from other parts of the face or 'mask' – was used from the mid-1800s onwards to form the body of a fly that was mentioned by Francis Francis, by James Ogden (who is sometimes credited as the creator of the GRHE) and by Frederic Halford, but in all these cases they were re-

'One of the best flies for bulging fish is the gold-ribbed hare's ear, and the reason is not far to seek. Put side by side…a nymph of one of the Ephemeridae and an artificial of the above pattern. It will at once be noted that there are arranged in pairs on the foremost segments of the abdomen of the nymph a number of fin-like appendages.... The short hairs of the fur picked out in the body of the artificial bear a strong resemblance to these branchiae.' **Frederic M. Halford, Dry-fly Fishing in Theory and Practice (1889)**

ferring to a winged blue dun. The wings were slips from a starling's wing feather; Ogden gave the fly a tail of three strands of a red cock's hackle and Halford gave it a red cock's beard hackle. Ogden, writing in 1879, recommended adding a tinge of olive colour to the hare's fur by using onion juice or by 'mixing with it a little olive fur from a monkey's neck', but that's no longer advisable! He also instructed the fly tyer to pick out the dubbing to form the legs and to rib the hare's ear body 'with fine gold tinsel or twist' for variety, advice that has been heeded by generations since.

This was clearly a wet fly, and Ogden tells us, 'When the season is mild this fly will be on the water by the end of February, and is most killing on cold days. When using them, allow your flies to sink a little, letting the water do the work; by no means hurrying or dragging them against the stream.'

According to Halford, writing in 1886, 'This is probably the most killing pattern of the present day in the Test and other

The combination of soft fur and stiff bristles make the hair of the hare's ears and mask ideal for dubbing nymph bodies that remain slightly spiky in the water.

chalk-streams; in fact, one of the most skilful and successful anglers in the county of Hants [Hampshire] scarcely ever uses any other dun, from the opening of the season in March until the closing of the river. It is equally efficacious for trout and grayling.'

REVERSING THE LIFE CYCLE

When exactly the winged dun became a wingless nymph is unclear. G.E.M. Skues, a dedicated nymph fisher, is said to have fished the winged hare's ear, but at a certain point a more 'buggy' and nymph-like wingless version made its debut. It has remained an essential in the fly box of every wet fly angler ever since.

The caddis larva is just one of the many aquatic invertebrates that the Hare's Ear Nymph, tied in various colours and sizes, represents so well.

Traditionally the tail of the nymph was made of long guard hairs from the hare's ear, but hen hackle and saddle feather fibres are now equally common. Gold wire for the rib is tied in, a tapered body of dubbed hare's fur is wrapped to just forward of the midpoint and the gold rib is counter wound and tied off. A bunch of pheasant or turkey tail fibres is tied in and a tight but spiky thorax of the same dubbing (often with additional guard hairs from the ears) is then wrapped. The tail fibres are pulled over the thorax to form the wing case, tied off behind the hook eye and whip finished. The crucial final step, as Ogden so rightly pointed out, is to pick out the fur of the thorax with a needle or dubbing brush to give the fly a shaggy and unruly appearance and create the nymph-like legs and branchiae that give it life in the water.

Tied using the natural hare's ear fur, this nymph represents many of the paler species of caddis and mayfly, but by using dyed and/or mixed furs and by varying the colour of the tail and wingcase and the size of the hook, the fly tyer can simulate an enormous range of nymphs covering not only many species of caddis and mayfly but also stoneflies, damsel- and dragonflies.

VARIATIONS ON THE HAIR'S EAR THEME

The Gold-Ribbed Hare's Ear Nymph can be, and is, fished anywhere in the water column, wrapping the hook with wire for a slow sink or, more commonly, adding a gold bead head to get down fast. At the other end of the spectrum, as an emerger pattern, there is a floating version with a tail and underbody of elk hair tied humpy style on a dry fly hook, and there is also a parachute hare's ear with a poly yarn post and a pale hackle wound horizontally.

For added sparkle, Flashabou can be added to the tail or used as a first rib under the gold wire, ice wing fibre can be mixed into the dubbing or laid over the wing case, which is then lacquered or coated with UV-setting clear finish, or flashback can be used in place of feather fibres to form the wing case. The Soft Hackle Hare's Ear Nymph, created by John Gierach, has a mottled hen or partridge hackle to add further movement in the water, and it works well during a caddis hatch.

And if that range of possibilities isn't enough, you can always go full circle and return to the original, the Gold-Ribbed Hare's Ear winged wet fly, which remains as popular and effective as it was in its heyday.

Some tyers add weight to the Hare's Ear Nymph by wrapping the hook shank with lead wire to get the fly down through the water column, but the same goal is commonly achieved by the addition of a gold bead head.

Bass Popper

YEAR: 1915   **FLY TYER:** Ernest Peckinpaugh   **LOCATION:** Tennessee, USA

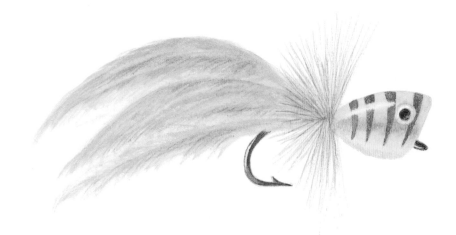

The Original Recipe

Hook
Long-shank hook, #1/0–#6

Tail
Marabou or saddle feathers

Thread
Green tying thread

Collar
Deer hair or saddle hackle

Body / Head
Shaped and painted cork

Light enough to be cast with a fly rod, heavy enough to create an impact when it hits the water and sculpted to create as much disturbance as possible when stripped across the surface, the Bass Popper has been with us for almost a century and its popularity continues to grow. Whether the term 'fly' can truly be applied to it is beside the point. The Bass Bug enables anglers to target predatory fish in difficult lies with dramatic effect.

BASS ON THE FLY

Given that largemouth, or black, bass can grow to more than 20lb (9kg), are aggressive feeders and ferocious fighters, it is hardly surprising that they quickly attracted the attention of the early North American fly fishers. Writing in 1892, Mary Orvis Marbury tells us that, 'In America, "fancy flies" are more numerous than the imitations, especially since their introduction as a lure for black bass'. Almost one third of all the colour plates in *Favorite Flies and Their Histories* depict large and brightly coloured bass flies, and salmon flies such as the Silver Doctor, the Kingfisher and the Parmacheene Belle were also considered very effective for bass when worked close to the surface.

However, a largemouth bass is not a salmon, and it fully deserves its name, as well as such nicknames as widemouth, bigmouth and bucketmouth. This is a fish that will consume frogs, bats, small birds and even baby alligators, and in 1907 Ernest Peckinpaugh – a building contractor and a keen bass fisherman from Chattanooga, Tennessee – came up with a way to offer it what it wanted on the end of a fly line.

Among the 60 bass flies illustrated in her book, Mary Orvis Marbury depicts the Golden Dustman, Henshall, Knight Templar, Jungle Cock (first tied by Charles Orvis in 1879), Holberton and Holberton II.

CONCEPT TO COMMERCE

The story goes that the cork from his bottle fell into the river while he was fishing. As it floated downstream he came up with the idea of a large, buoyant 'fly', and he soon made a prototype consisting of a cork with a long hook through it and two bunches of deer hair at the head. Crude though it was, it worked on the bream for which he was fishing, and he soon discovered that the voracious and highly territorial bass would go for it too. Over the next few years Ernest experimented with shaping the body, varying the size, and using feather and deer hair in different ways to refine what was proving to be a very successful fly, the flat or concave face of the design creating a popping sound on the surface that proved so attractive to the warm water predators. Friends and local fishing guides had equal success with it, and some examples of Ernest's craftsmanship fell into the hands of writer, outdoorsman and conservationist Will H. Dilg, who was so impressed that he had a local tyer make some copies and develop new models. When he wrote about the new flies in national magazines it created such a demand for these 'bugs' that Ernest was virtually forced to begin commercial production in order to protect his own interests, and the E.H. Peckinpaugh Company went into business in 1920.

The demand for Ernest H. Peckinpaugh's new creation soon transformed his hobby into a full-scale business venture as established tackle manufacturers cashed in on the idea.

BOOM, BUST AND BOOM

'Peck's Poppers' were the start of a new genre of flies that were to multiply and diversify rapidly. Many manufacturing companies sprang up in the 1920s and 1930s, selling literally hundreds of thousands of the new bugs. The creations sprouted tails and wings, fins and legs, and there was a move

towards using more feather and bucktail with clipped deer hair for the heads, and giving the bugs a more streamlined profile that would cast more easily, but the essential principles remained the same. The flat-faced poppers were joined by more bullet-shaped sliders, skippers with a steeply angled face that causes the bug to jump along the water, and darters and divers that have a jutting lower lip to pull the bug under the surface. By the 1940s Peckinpaugh and his 300-strong team of fly tyers were turning out some 60 types of bass bugs and flies in various colour combinations, but there was a downturn on the way. From the end of the Second World War right through the 1960s spinners and spinning rods were all the rage, and bass bugging went into decline.

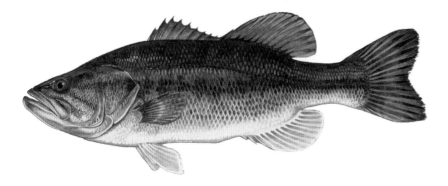

It wasn't until the 1970s that fly fishing for bass, promoted by innovative fly tyers such as Dave Whitlock (see page 151 [Dave's Hopper]), creator of the Hairbug and many other deer hair flies, began to make a comeback. It is now the fastest growing area of the sport in North America, influencing fly fishing methods for predatory fish in fresh- and saltwater around the world.

FISHING THE BUG

Poppers are particularly well suited to largemouth bass because these fish frequently feed at the surface and hunt by sound as well as by sight. Designed to represent any potential food item – from a fish to a frog, from a snake to a salamander – bass bugs are generally cast to structure that may be harbouring large fish and are presented with as much splash as possible to attract attention. The fly is often left to rest for a few seconds while the ripples die away and then given a series of short, sharp strips, causing a noisy commotion on the surface as the water is thrown up by the face of the popper. Takes are typically explosive, which explains why the sport has such a following.

The size of the popper needs to be tailored to the fish (smaller bugs for smallmouth bass, for example), to the water conditions (larger poppers in rough water in order to make plenty of noise) and to the feeding style of the fish (larger poppers are more successful with more voracious fish).

Bass bugs will also take pike and, in suitable sizes, peacock bass in the Amazon, freshwater dorado and South African yellowfish, as well as saltwater species such as striped bass, yellowtail kingfish and barramundi.

Aggressive and voracious, and found in almost every kind of freshwater habitat, bass, both largemouth (above) and smallmouth, are the number one sportfish in North America, and an ever increasing number of anglers are discovering the thrill of using a fly rod to catch them.

Adams

YEAR: 1922   **FLY TYER:** Leonard Halladay   **LOCATION:** Mayfield, Michigan, USA

The **Original Recipe**

Hook
Dry fly hook, #8–#14 or smaller

Thread
Grey tying thread

Wings
Grizzly hackle tips

Tail
Golden pheasant tippet fibres

Body
Grey yarn

Hackle
One grizzly and one brown
hackle feather

Most North American fly fishers would agree that if you were only able to use one dry fly pattern for the rest of your life, it would have to be the Adams. Often called the most effective pattern ever tied, this buoyant grey and brown mayfly / caddis / you-name-it imitation marks another page in American fly-fishing history.

The individual history of the Adams itself is surprisingly well known, and the fly's origin can be pinned down to a summer's day in 1922, when one Charles F. Adams and his son Lon (both of them attorneys from Ohio) returned from a morning's trout fishing on the Boardman River in northern Michigan. Frustrated at being unable to match the hatch that had been taking place, Charles visited his old friend and fishing companion Leonard Halladay in the nearby village of Mayfield. Len, a keen angler and a local guide, had been tying flies for more than 30 years, and Charles thought he could provide the solution. He wasn't mistaken.

Whether Charles gave Len samples of the rogue fly or just a verbal description of it is unclear, but the outcome was a chunky fly with a golden pheasant tippet tail, a body of grey yarn, a pair of forward slanted grizzly wings and a palmered brown and grizzly hackle.

'The first Adams I made I handed to Mr. Adams who was fishing in a small pond in front of my house, to try on the Boardman that evening. When he came back next morning, he wanted to know what I called it. He said it was a "knock-out" and I said we would call it the Adams, since he had made the first good catch on it.' **Len Halladay quoted in Harold Hinsdill Smedley's** ***Fly Patterns and Their Origins* (1944)**

By varying the colour of the body and the size of the hook from a #14 to as large as a #8, the Adams can represent anything from a blue wing olive through Callibaetis *dun to a grey or green drake or even the gigantic* Hexagenia *mayfly.*

The modern Adams generally has a yarn body and long, slim, upright wings, with a tail of hackle fibres.

RAPID MUTATION

The fly's reputation spread quickly but, despite its evident success, the pattern was soon amended. Within a couple of years, dubbed muskrat fur was substituted for the grey wool yarn, simply because fur gave the fly greater buoyancy. Then, in the early 1930s, as the Adams made its way eastwards, it fell under the influence of the Catskill fly tyers. In keeping with their style, the forward-swept upright wings were pulled back and spread apart, while the body itself was trimmed to a sleeker outline. By the end of the 1930s, the tail, too, had been changed, the pheasant tippet fibres being replaced with brown and grizzly hackle fibres, the same materials as the palmered hackle. While versions close to the original can still be found, the commercially available Adams generally incorporates most, if not all, of these changes.

PARACHUTING IN

The universal qualities of this fly have made it a popular choice for tying in different styles and with various materials. Many types of fly are tied with a parachute hackle, but the Parachute Adams is probably the most famous and one of the most productive of these. The key feature is an upright wing of white calf hair or a synthetic material such as Antron®. The grizzly and brown hackle is then tied around the base of this wing. This creates a highly visible fly that sits with its body in the surface film rather than held above the surface, and the fibres of the horizontal hackle look like legs spread flat on the water. The overall impression is of an emerging dun struggling out of the nymphal shuck, of an egg-laying female or of a dead or dying spinner, all of which are tempting food items for the fish. The parachute hackle is also aptly named, as it causes the fly to land gently on the water the right way up.

The horizontal hackle spiralling around an upright wing post gives the Parachute Adams its delicate presentation.

THE IRRESISTIBLE FLY

The buoyant qualities of deer hair are used in countless flies, but the Irresistible is a way of tying that can be applied to many patterns. The style was developed by Joe Messinger of West Virginia in the 1930s, giving a mayfly pattern a body of clipped spun deer hair to form what he initially called the Deer Hair Drake, which soon became the Irresistible. Harry Darbee independently tied a similar fly with grizzly hackle tip wings and a ginger hackle in the late 1930s that he called the Beaverhead Bastard (being the unlikely progeny of a bass bug and a trout fly), but that didn't have the right tone for a commercial fly (Woolly Bugger is bad enough) and a friend's daughter suggested Rat-Faced McDougall. The grizzly wings were changed to wings of white calf tail at the request of a customer who needed greater visibility. It wasn't long before the Adams became the recipient of the spun deer hair treatment, creating the Adams Irresistible, a high-floating fly that excels in a range of sizes on fast flowing and rough water.

The original Irresistible, the Rat-faced McDougall and the Adams Irresistible all share the same highly buoyant spun deer hair body, making them ideal for rapid and tumbling water.

ADAM AND EVE

Another popular variation on the Adams is the Lady, or Female, Adams, tied with an egg sac of yellow dubbing at the tail to represent an egg-laying female. On a similar theme, the Yellow Adams is tied like the standard fly but with a body made entirely of yellow dry fly dubbing to simulate hatches of the Sulphur and Cahill mayflies.

The Female Adams, with its yellow tag behind the grey yarn body, represents a mayfly laying her eggs through the surface film.

Gray Ghost

YEAR: 1924   **FLY TYER:** Carrie G. Stevens   **LOCATION:** Maine, USA

The Original Recipe

Hook
Extra long streamer hook, #4

Thread
White and black tying thread

Body
Orange silk floss ribbed with
silver tinsel

Underbelly
4–6 peacock eye fibres and
white bucktail

Throat
Golden pheasant crest

Wing
Golden pheasant crest and
4 hackles

Shoulders and cheeks
Silver pheasant and jungle cock

Head
Black with orange band

The use of feathers in simple streamer patterns for sea fishing probably dates back hundreds of years, but the development of complex and artistic freshwater forms really begins in the USA at the start of the 20th century, reaching a first peak in the hands of tyers in the state of Maine. Using her own unique tying methods, Carrie G. Stevens of Upper Dam created a series of long, streamlined, composite-wing streamers, of which her Gray Ghost is the best known.

THE NEW ENGLAND SCHOOL

Besides his iconic Quill Gordon and a host of other dry flies, Theodore Gordon's Bumblepuppy – more of a template than a single pattern – was a trendsetter, combining feathers with the more commonly used bucktail of the time and taking the first steps towards the modern feather streamer fly.

The theme was picked up by the Maine tyers, who developed the distinctive New England streamer style through the 1920s and 1930s. These tyers included: Herbie Welch, whose Black Ghost, with its long white hackle and jungle cock cheeks, is world famous; Bill Edson, whose Light and Dark Edson Tigers had reflective metal cheeks; and Joe Stickney, who designed the Supervisor (he was a Supervisor of Wardens for Saco, Maine) to represent the smelt on which brook trout feed. Not being a fly tyer, Stickney commissioned others to execute his design, and one of these was Carrie Stevens.

Through its writers, editors and photographers, Field & Stream *has been taking – and quickening – the pulse of fly fishing in the USA since 1895, making it the oldest continually published sporting magazine in North America.*

CARRIE GERTRUDE STEVENS

Her flies, with a distinctive band around the head, were generally longer and slimmer than those of her colleagues. Stevens not only constructed the wing assemblies before tying them on, attaching the jungle cock cheeks using lacquer, but she also tied the wings parallel along the sides of the hook rather than in the more common tented fashion, reducing the width of the streamer.

She first tied the Gray Ghost in 1924, and immediately caught a 6lb 13oz (2.8kg) brook trout on it that took second prize in a *Field & Stream* contest. It was the best advertising she could have had, and she could barely keep up with orders for the new fly. Her style is still influencing streamer tyers today.

Gray Wulff

YEAR: 1929   **FLY TYER:** Lee Wulff   **LOCATION:** New York State, USA

The Original Recipe

Hook
Dry fly, #4–#18

Wing
Brown bucktail fibres

Thread
Black tying thread

Body
Dubbed muskrat fur

Tail
Brown bucktail fibres

Hackle
Dark dun hackle

The initial development of the fly tying tradition in the USA took place largely to adapt British patterns to represent North American insects and partly to incorporate locally available materials, but one man found other good reasons to innovate. Lee Wulff, who was to have an impact on so many aspects of fishing, wanted flies that would float better and last longer on the tumbling freestone streams and rivers that he fished, and he also wanted to offer the trout a more substantial mouthful. The Gray Wulff, first tied during a stay in the Adirondacks in 1929, was not so much a new fly as a new way of tying.

BEEFING IT UP

'Each fly is a dream we cast out to fool fish.' **Lee Wulff**

All the dry flies at the time were tied with wings and tails of feather, and because these are not naturally very buoyant the flies had to be light and, in Lee's opinion, insubstantial. He wanted a material that was durable, floated higher in the water, had more bulk and was highly visible, and he found what he was looking for in bucktail — the brown and white hair from the tail of the white-tailed deer. Using brown bucktail for the tail and wing (his original pattern has a single upright wing), dubbed muskrat fur for the body and a medium blue dun hackle, he created a fly that imitates many darker mayflies but especially the gray and green drakes of the Catskills and Adirondacks.

In this 1880s lithograph, an angler plays a fish below rapids on the Raquette River in New York State's Adirondack Mountains, where Lee developed his innovative pattern.

The fly was an instant success and it clearly had the durability he sought, as he reportedly landed more than fifty trout on the same fly in one outing.

THE WULFF PACK

At the same time, Lee also tied the White Wulff to imitate paler mayflies, using the white bucktail, white fur dubbing and a silver badger hackle (white with a black line down the centre). His fishing partner Dan Bailey created the Grizzly Wulff, with grizzly and brown hackles and a yellow floss body for use in Wyoming. It was he who, recognising the commercial potential of the new fly design, chose to split the hair wing, feeling it would have a more popular appearance, and Wulff incorporated this change into his own style.

Lee Wulff himself saw his creation as a general pattern, rather than a specific fly, and history has borne this out, his basic concept lending itself to such variations as the Black Wulff, Brown Wulff, Blonde Wulff and Royal Wulff.

For many Wulff flies bucktail has been replaced by moose, elk and calf hair in a range of colours, and the original muskrat fur body of the Gray Wulff has been changed to dubbing, floss and yarn of various kinds to simulate a range of may and other flies. The wings and tail of the Montana Wulff, for example, are red squirrel hair, and the body is olive-green dubbed fur. Gary LaFontaine's Were Wulff (one of more than 60 patterns attributed to him) has a tail of brown calf tail and a white calf tail wing with a dubbed hare's ear body. LaFontaine described it as having 'an Adams for a mother and a Hare's Ear for a father'.

EXTENDING THE RANGE

The view from below shows how high this style of fly floats on the water, the tail of bucktail fibres leaving a strong impression on the surface.

Intending it as a trout fly, Lee initially tied the Wulff pattern in fairly small sizes, but it wasn't long before he took larger versions with him on salmon fishing trips to Nova Scotia, and later to Newfoundland and Labrador. The fly again proved its worth and Lee Wulff became a leading proponent of dry fly fishing for salmon, pioneering the use of shorter, single-handed rods – as short as 6ft (1.8m) – and revolutionising the sport in North America. Taking short rods to their logical extreme, he is said to have landed a 10lb (4.5kg) salmon on just a reel with no rod at all!

Nor are Wulff flies restricted to fast and rocky rivers, to game fish or to North America. These flies are now used worldwide and are fished on still waters, slow and smooth waters, and on limestone creeks and rivers. They will also often tempt a bass.

Lee Wulff

The man whose commitment and innovation were to transform so many aspects of sport fishing started life in Alaska, where his father was seeking his fortune in the Gold Rush. The family moved to Brooklyn when he was 10 years old, and he soon began exploring the fishing potential of New York State. After a brief period spent studying engineering he moved to Paris to attend art college, and on his return to New York he joined an advertising agency, while still spending as much time as he could trout fishing.

He then went freelance and built a career that was centred on his passion for fishing, setting up fishing camps in Newfoundland and Labrador and gaining his pilot's licence so that he could search for remote fishing locations by float plane. Turning his hand to writing, he contributed articles and illustrations to magazines and in 1939 he published his *Handbook of Freshwater Fishing*, in which he outlined the principles of 'catch and release' for which he became a leading advocate, coining the slogan, 'Game fish are too valuable to be caught only once'.

Taking up photography and film making, Wulff was involved in the production of the television series *The American Sportsman*, which he used to publicise the importance of fish and habitat protection. It was during the filming of one episode that he met Joan Salvato, America's pre-eminent fly caster. They were married in 1967 and together founded the Joan and Lee Wulff Fishing School on the Beaverkill River.

MASTER OF INNOVATION

Anglers can thank Lee Wulff for a great deal more than just his flies. In 1931 he came up with the idea of the fishing vest, sewing the prototype himself. Short enough to stay dry while wading and with enough pockets to carry everything you need, it soon became an essential part of the fly fisher's kit. He later developed the cageless reel that could be palmed to increase drag, and promoted the left-hand wind reel, maintaining that the right-handed angler should hold the rod in the stronger hand. The triangle taper fly line, which has been taken up by many manufacturers, was another Wulff invention.

In 1990, at the age of 85, he was still fishing and catching monster marlin, but the following year he died while flying a light aircraft to renew his pilot's licence. It is thought that he suffered a heart attack. Both he and his wife Joan have since been inducted into the Hall of Fame of the International Game Fish Association.

Even when he was in his 70s Lee Wulff remained a master at tying flies in the hand without the use of a vice.

Prince Nymph

YEAR: 1930s   **FLY TYER:** Don and Dick Olson   **LOCATION:** Minnesota, USA

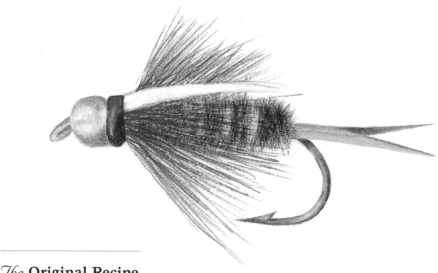

The Original Recipe

Hook
2XL nymph, #10–#16

Body
Peacock herl

Thread
Black tying thread

Rib
Fine gold tinsel

Head
Brass bead

Hackle
Brown hen hackle

Tail
Brown goose biots

Wings
White goose biots

Whether it should be considered an attractor pattern or an imitation of a stonefly, caddis or other nymph, the Prince is right up there alongside the Hare's Ear and the Pheasant Tail as an all-time favourite. A direct descendant of the Zug Bug, which has a peacock sword tail and mallard feather wing case, the Prince has the same gold-ribbed peacock herl body and soft hackle but has a pair of brown goose biot tails and white goose biot wings.

THE FLY FORMERLY KNOWN AS...

Versions of its origins vary, but it was probably first tied in the 1930s by Don and Dick Olson of Minnesota, who called it the Brown Fork-Tailed Nymph. The fly was later made popular by Doug Prince of California, and when it appeared in a catalogue in the 1940s it did so under the name we now know it by.

Be that as it may, it works well in the kind of fast water that stoneflies love, with a lead wire wrap to give it sinkability, and bead-head versions are now more common than the original. One theory holds that the white biots might represent the stringy remains of the wing case seen on *Isonychia* mayfly nymphs, which are common in the US Midwest (hence the Minnesota connection), but they may just add visibility and the pattern seems to work well almost everywhere, in still waters as well as rivers, and for many fish species besides trout.

THE UNSUNG BARB

Given the versatility and availability of biots, it's surprising that they are not more widely used. Biots are the relatively stiff, flat barbs on the leading edge of a bird's primary feathers, and white goose biots are the most commonly used, often dyed in a range of colours. Turkey biots are longer and wider but tend to be stiffer, while those of the duck and ring-neck hen pheasant are smaller but softer.

In various sizes and colours, biots can be used to form tails, wing cases, legs and antennae, but they can also be wrapped around the hook shank to form a realistically segmented body (ridged or smooth, depending on which side of the biot is outermost) on smaller flies such as midge pupae and even small dries.

Muddler Minnow

YEAR: 1936   **FLY TYER:** Don Gapen   **LOCATION:** Ontario, Canada

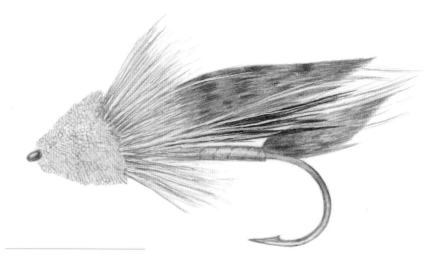

The Original Recipe

Hook
Wet fly, #2–#10

Thread
Yellow tying thread

Tail
Matched slips of mottled
turkey quill

Body
Flat gold braid or tinsel

Underwing
Squirrel fur or calf tail

Overwing
Matched slips of mottled
turkey quill

Collar
Natural deer hair tips

Head
Spun and trimmed natural
deer hair

When Don Gapen first tied this fly in his camp beside the Nipigon River, he could hardly have imagined that it would become one of the world's best known streamer patterns, nor that his basic idea would be taken up by so many fly tyers and lead to such a wide array of flies representing every subsurface food item, from a nymph to a large baitfish, as well as floating terrestrials.

BORN TO FISH

There was never any doubt that Don would be a keen angler, being brought up on the Gateway Lodge beside Hungry Jack Lake, just off the Gunflint Trail in the north-eastern wilderness of Minnesota. The resort, one of the biggest and best in the state in the 1920s, was built by Don's parents, Jesse and Sue Gapen, and for hundreds of anglers it was indeed a gateway — to the fishing experience of a lifetime, casting for lake trout, northern pike and land-locked salmon. (Jesse Gapen also introduced small-mouth bass to the region, where they have flourished.)

In 1936 the family purchased a second resort, the Chalet Bungalow Lodge on the Nipigon River in Ontario, and Don moved to Canada to run it. Here double-figure brook trout could be added to the list of target fish, and Don soon discovered that the First Nations people used the small sculpin minnows, known locally as 'cockatush', as bait for the big fish. Catching a few of these baitfish himself, he proceeded to tie a dozen sculpin patterns of his own design, and the following day he tried them out. The Muddler Minnow was born.

REFINED AND RENOWNED

Although the basic ingredients of those first flies were the same as those used in the standard Muddler today, Don's original version, tied on a #2 hook, was a fairly scruffy affair by comparison. With a tail of brown mottled turkey wing feather, gold tinsel wrapped around the hook shank and a central tuft of grey squirrel tail hair between two mottled turkey wing feather slips for the body, his fly had a broad, shaggy head of spun deer hair — and it was astoundingly effective, not just for the brook trout

The mottled turkey quill is a signature element in the Muddler Minnow and its many descendants.

(in 1939 Don Gapen took a 10lb 4oz (4.7kg) brookie from the Nipigon River on a Muddler) but also for bass, walleye and pike.

The Muddler Minnow caught the fishing public's imagination when the angling writer Joe Brooks, who had had great success with the fly, extolled its virtues in a magazine article, calling it the best all-round fly of its kind. Brooks also showed the fly to Dan Bailey, the owner of a fly shop and commercial fly-tying business in Livingston, on the Yellowstone River in Montana, where Brooks had a summer home, and Bailey began experimenting with variations on the pattern, in particular trimming the head to a neat profile, leaving a hackle of longer deer hair. Soon it was in full-scale production, and this is the look that we now associate with this fly. In the 1950s the fly shop was already becoming known by the many East Coast anglers who were following Joe Brooks's lead and coming to Montana to fish but now, with Brooks's help, Bailey and the Muddler Minnow really brought each other into the spotlight. The fly soon achieved enormous popularity across North America.

FURTHER CHANGES

The trimmed spun deer hair head is the constant theme in the Muddler family, but there have been literally hundreds of variations since the early days. Dan Bailey was responsible for several of these. In addition to the new, neater version of the original, he also created what was initially called the White Muddler, a ghostly white cross between Gapen's Muddler and Theodore Gordon's Bumblepuppy. It was soon renamed the Missoulian Spook by cartoonist Vince Hamlin, who had considerable success with it and featured it in one of his sketches. (Missoula is a town on the Clark Fork River in Montana.)

Bailey also created a version in which the turkey feather wings were replaced by marabou, and another called the Spuddler, supposedly because its hackle feather wings were similar to those of a West Coast fly called the Spruce Streamer.

By the 1960s the Muddler Minnow had gained popularity around the world, but especially in Europe, New Zealand (where cicada-pattern and rabbit-fur Muddlers are fished) and Australia, where the Missoulian Spook made its arrival in the late 1950s followed closely by the Muddler Minnow itself. In the Antipodes it was adapted to represent the local prey fish using, among many others, marabou versions in black, yellow and olive as well as a splendid Matuka pattern (see page 128).

Originally designed to be fished on a sinking line close to the bottom, simulating the behaviour of the sculpin, bullhead and other small fish, Don Gapen's fly had a loose deer hair head, but because the head is now tied much more densely it is more buoyant. This makes it easier to fish in the upper layers and on the surface, where it can be extremely effective stripped noisily like a bass bug. Sinking versions are usually weighted with lead wire or a brass cone head.

The Muddler Minnow successfully represents many small freshwater fish, including the juveniles of catfish such as the black bullhead, as well as saltwater baitfish.

The pattern seems to have that 'general' look that enables it to mimic many different food items simply by changes in colour and size, and by using the appropriate line, from full sink to floating, in still waters, rivers, estuaries and open ocean. As well as its role as a bait fish, in smaller sizes it can be fished as a nymph, as a dry sedge or a hopper. There are versions for sea trout, steelhead and salmon, and in large sizes it has taken saltwater fish including bonefish, bonita, crevalle jacks and snook. The Tarpon Muddler has a full marabou body and tail, a slim deer hair head and hackle – and nothing else.

British Columbia has its own Rolled Muddler, a small baitfish pattern with a silver tinsel body, feather fibre tail and wing with a Flashabou overwing, and a slim head and collar of deer hair, fished in estuaries and off the beaches for cutthroat trout, coho and pink salmon.

The Unstoppable Lodge

The original fishing lodge built by Jesse Gapen on Hungry Jack Lake was destroyed by fire in 1931, but was rebuilt within a year. In 1972, under new ownership, it burnt down again; a new log building was transported to the site, and it was open for business by the end of the following year. The lodge was completely destroyed by fire yet again in the spring of 2008 but was up again and running within 20 months, and the Hungry Jack Lodge Resort and Campground is still going strong.

Tom Thumb

YEAR: 1930s   **FLY TYER:** Anon.   **LOCATION:** Britain and British Columbia, Canada

The Original Recipe

Hook
1 or 2XL wet fly, #10–#16

Body
Deer hair

Thread
Red tying thread

Wing
Deer hair

Tail
Deer hair

Simple materials, easy construction, excellent buoyancy and a great profile on the water have made the Tom Thumb a favourite fly with many anglers on both rivers and still waters. Described by educator and conservationist Ralph Shaw as 'the dry for all seasons', it can represent a wide diversity of insects throughout the year.

This fly may have originated on both sides of the Atlantic independently. Historically, the Algonquin First Nations of the north-eastern USA and eastern Canada may have used a similar deer hair fly, and it is certain that this exact pattern was being sold in Britain in the early 1940s, probably made with the hair of the red deer. At the same time it made its appearance in western Canada, where there is plenty of deer hair, and it has become one of the most famous flies in British Columbia and western Alberta.

In essence the fly is just two bunches of deer hair, one tied in to form the upward-angled tail and a second, longer bunch tied in, also butt forwards, and then folded forward to form the shell back with the hair tips forming a fan-like semi-circular wing. In Canada the preferred deer hair is that of the coastal blacktail deer taken early in the season. The coastal deer hair lacks the marked black tips of hair from deer in the colder interior, and in the early season the hair tends to be finer and more even, making it easier to use on smaller hooks. The hair of yearling elk can be used for paler patterns, and Tom Thumbs are also tied in black, dark brown and even green.

The hair of the indigenous red deer was formerly used in Europe to tie the Tom Thumb. The fly remains popular for grayling and trout on fast-flowing water.

SIZE IS THE KEY

In various sizes from a #16 to a #10, a Tom Thumb can suggest anything from an emerging chironomid, through mayflies, ants and water boatmen to caddis flies (steelhead anglers have been known to fish a #8 or even a #6 as a skating fly) but matching the size to the circumstances is of prime importance. In the smaller sizes, on still water, it is best fished on a floating line and a long leader cast among, or ahead of, feeding trout and then left at rest, but in its finest incarnation – as an emerging travelling sedge up to 1in (2.5cm) long – retrieving it across the surface with a halting, skittering motion can elicit fierce takes. Such takes reveal the fly's weakness, namely that the deer-hair shell back is vulnerable to being frayed and cut by teeth, but even a dishevelled fly seems to attract the fish. Some tyers coat the shell back with varnish to lengthen its life.

The buoyancy of this fly also allows it to be fished with a full-sinking line and a relatively short leader to mimic scuds and small pupae close to the bottom without hooking up in the weed.

THE HUMPY

In about 1940, when the Tom Thumb was first having an impact in Canada, a very similar fly was being designed by Jack Horner in the Northern Sierra of California for the fast-flowing Truckee River. Tied in much the same way as the Tom Thumb – with a tail, shell back and wings all of deer hair – it also has a good deal in common with the Wulff flies, having a split wing and a hackle tied behind and in front of the wings. Given the natural buoyancy of the deer hair, the hackle is not required for support and can be sparse. The result is a fly that rides the western streams as well as the Wulff rides the less turbulent rivers of the Catskills.

The fly was at first known, logically enough, as Horner's Deer Hair Fly in California, but by 1943 it had crossed the Rockies and reached Montana, where it was renamed the Goofus Bug. The two names were used in the two regions until the late 1940s,, when the term Humpy was applied in Wyoming and that is the name by which it is now known

An angler casts a fly onto the ruffled waters of the Truckee near Reno, Nevada. Jack Horner designed his deer hair fly to fish this river further upstream in California.

everywhere. The term Goofus Bug is still sometimes used to refer to a version with a brown and a grizzly hackle. The Humpy remains near the top of the dry angler's list of favourites in the western USA and up into Canada.

HUMPY VARIATIONS

The development of the Humpy has taken two main directions: changes to the kinds of hair used in the tying, and the addition of a floss or thread underbody in a range of colours.

The Royal Humpy, which has also been attributed to Charlie Ridenour of Wyoming, is a highly visible fly with the same sartorial elegance as its cousin, the Royal Wulff.

The fly was largely popularised by Wyoming fly tyer and author Jack Dennis, who replaced the deer hair with elk hair in the 1960s and gave the fly a black elk hair tail. Elk hair is now commonly used to tie the Humpy, being more durable than deer hair. Dennis also developed the popular Royal Humpy, which has a red floss underbody and white calf hair wings in the style of the Royal Wulff, and this is the fly that featured on the front cover of his *Western Trout Fly Tying Manual*, published in 1974.

Other members of the group include the Wood-Duck Humpy, with wings of wood-duck flank and looking rather like a Quill Gordon on steroids, and the PT Humpy, with bundled pheasant tail fibres for the body and wing – a good-looking fly but lacking the buoyancy of the original.

In the early 1980s another Wyoming fly tyer, Joe Allen, came up with the double Humpy (whether by accident or design is unclear), an effective pattern comprising two Humpies on the same shank.

DESIGNER HUMPIES

The Yellow Humpy, with a yellow floss body, is a good representation of yellow mayflies such as the Little Yellow Sally, and of yellow and golden stoneflies. A green floss body is another popular variation. The Adams Humpy, with a grey body and a brown and grizzly hackle, is also a good mayfly pattern, and the Black Humpy is an effective beetle imitation.

The colour variations are endless, but the most recent developments have been in the use of synthetic materials. Humpies now exist that retain the essential design but incorporate diverse elements such as foam bodies, poly yarn wings and rubber legs, widening yet further the already extensive range of situations in which this versatile fly will catch, on still waters as well as rivers.

Flymph

YEAR: 1941   **FLY TYER:** James Leisenring   **LOCATION:** Pennsylvania, USA

The Original Recipe

Hook
1XL nymph, #12–#16

Body
Hare's ear blend on waxed
silk dubbing loop

Thread
Waxed grey tying silk

Hackle
Hungarian partridge
soft hackle

Developed in the 1930s and 1940s by Jim Leisenring and Vernon S. 'Pete' Hidy, flymphs represent the next stage in the evolution of the soft-hackled fly, following in the footsteps of the British North Country fly tyers and G.E.M. Skues. Leisenring himself referred to his creations as 'wingless wets', and the term 'flymph' was later coined by Hidy to denote a specific way of representing the stage of development between the wingless nymph and the winged adult fly – in other words, an emerger.

TAKING IT FURTHER

James Leisenring, of Allentown, Pennsylvania, was well versed in the history of the soft-hackled wet flies that represent emerging insects such as caddis, mayfly and stonefly, with evident legs but as yet no visible wings, and he no doubt appreciated Skues's concept of 'kick', the enticing pulsing action of the hackle fibres in the current. (He and Skues corresponded with each other; Skues later gave a presentation of some of Leisenring's flies to the Flyfishers' Club in London, and Leisenring has since been called 'the American Skues'.) Leisenring certainly knew how effective the soft-hackled wets can be and how valuable they are, both for matching various stages of the hatch and as more general impressionistic patterns when there is no particular hatch taking place, but he also saw that there could be more to the soft-hackled fly than just the hackle.

The stonefly, as both a nymph and an adult (pictured below), is an important food item that is all too often ignored by the angler.

As we have seen, flies such as Stewart's Spider and the Partridge and Orange are little more than a thin thread body and a sparse hackle. Skues then beefed things up a bit by creating more of a thorax, and indeed he referred to some of his creations as 'soft-hackled thorax nymphs'. James Leisenring admired both these kinds of fly, describing Stewart's Spiders as 'a deadly combination on every stream I have ever fished', and developing his own version of Skues's beloved Tup's Indispensable, but he also took the soft hackle concept a stage further.

Leisenring observed that nymphs rising up through the water column contain small amounts of gas trapped beneath the exoskeleton, helping them to rise in the water and presumably helping the fly within to begin freeing itself from what will become the nymphal shuck. The gas gives the rising nymph a degree of translucency (a quality that Skues had earlier commented on in the context of Tup's Indispensable), and in his efforts to

The Great Collaboration

James Leisenring (1878–1951) was in his late fifties when he met Vernon S. 'Pete' Hidy, who was some 30 years his junior, while fishing in Pennsylvania. Hidy was very impressed with the flies that Leisenring had developed, and he proceeded to work with him on the production of a book about the 'wingless wets' and Leisenring's methods of fishing them. Entitled *The Art of Tying the Wet Fly*, it was published in 1941, and it is unlikely that the book would have seen the light of day had it not been for Hidy's commitment. In it Leisenring made a strong case for wingless wets being more effective than winged wet flies, as they more realistically represent the pre-adult transitional stages of the insect. After the death of James Leisenring in 1951, Pete Hidy continued to fish, develop and write about wingless wets. Thanks to Hidy's commitment, 1971 saw the publication of an updated and expanded edition of the

1941 volume with the title of *The Art of Tying the Wet Fly and Fishing the Flymph*. It contained three extra chapters on Hidy's fishing methods and it brought his term 'flymph' into general use. Further articles and chapters followed, and through his writings Pete Hidy gave wingless wet fly fishing a further lease on life at a time when the angling world was more willing to read, learn and experiment than it had been when Leisenring's book first appeared, just as America was entering the Second World War.

Pete Hidy, who was a founding member of the Flyfishers' Club of Oregon, died in 1983, and his son Lance continues to promote and extend the good work done by his father and James Leisenring.

James Leisenring's flies and his methods of fishing them have proved to be extremely effective.

simulate this Leisenring placed even greater emphasis on the body of the fly, experimenting with combinations of materials to achieve a naturalistic look, as well as using various soft hackles to give his flies that lifelike action in the water.

What's more, he developed flies that, although they were derived from the British traditions, were designed to represent specifically North American insects, and as a result his 'wingless wets' helped to stem a tide that had been flowing in favour of the dry fly in the USA for several decades.

KEEPING THE CONTRAST

James Leisenring's flies generally have dubbed bodies of natural materials. Although he did sometimes use bronze peacock herl or black herl from various birds, the majority are of furs such as hare's mask, mole, muskrat and squirrel that not only produce a shaggy appearance (especially those that have guard hairs) and but also take up water and retain small bubbles of air. These qualities create a fly that has a mobile surface, sinks quickly and has a slight gleam to it.

Mole's fur is fine and soft, and ideal for touch dubbing. It allows the colour of the thread to show through and therefore works well for flymphs.

To add to the translucent effect, Leisenring came up with a way to ensure that the waxed silk around which the dubbing was wrapped would remain visible, referring to the colour of the silk as the 'undercolour' and choosing colours carefully to complement the dubbing in realistic combinations.

Rather than twisting the dubbing material around a single thread or even using a dropped dubbing loop while tying the fly, he prepared dubbing loop bodies on waxed silk separately in advance and stored them on notched celluloid cards for later use. When the dubbing loop is wound around the hook shank to create a fairly bulky and fuzzy fly, the thread 'undercolour' can be seen clearly, giving the body both segmentation and an extra degree of three-dimensionality. Using pre-spun bodies has several advantages, making it easier to experiment with different colour combinations and to achieve consistent body construction.

Clark's Block

Leisenring made each pre-dubbed body by placing a section of waxed silk on his thigh, spreading the dubbing on it, folding the rest of the silk over it and then twisting the threads together, but Richard Clark, a friend of Leisenring and Hidy, came up with a more manageable method. Clark's Spinning Block consists of a smooth hardwood block with a bevelled edge at one end with a headless brass tack driven into the centre of the bevel, a notch at the other end and a notch on one side. A length of silk is run from the end notch, around the nail at the other end, and then trapped in the side notch. Dubbing material is than laid out on the silk, the end is released from the side notch and placed over the dubbing, and the silk can then be lifted off and twisted to form a dubbing rope.

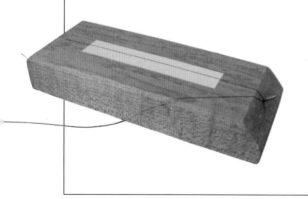

GETTING THE KICK

Of course, the hackle remains an essential element of this type of fly and, with his keen powers of observation and artistic sensibility for light and colour, Leisenring chose his hackles carefully. Using soft, webby and fairly thick fibres from the feathers of game birds such as partridge, woodcock and quail, as well as hen and starling, the collar hackle is often wound palmer-fashion down the first third or half of the hook shank, giving a more faithful representation of legs and other appendages.

To make sure the hackle feather is secure, it is tied in before the dubbing body is wound on and is left unwrapped until the thorax is completed. The relatively bulky thorax keeps the hackle fibres pushed out, in the same way as Skues's thread wraps behind the hackle, ensuring that the fibres will pulse with the current or the action of the retrieve.

As a wet fly will commonly revolve to some degree on the end of the line, flymphs are tied 'in the round', with no top or bottom. Without wing cases or a specific underside there is no upside-down position that might look unnatural in the water.

FISHING THE FLYMPH

In keeping with his aim of creating a lifelike fly that had a natural movement in the water, James Leisenring developed a technique to produce the behaviour of an ascending nymph. Known as the Leisenring Lift, the technique is generally used when fishing across and downstream with the fly close to the riverbed. At the end of the drift, once the line and leader are straight, the tip of the rod is raised, increasing the pressure of the current on the line and, in Leisenring's own words, 'causing the fly to lift from the bottom and rise with the hackles or legs quivering after the manner of the hatching natural fly'.

A similar technique can be used when fishing upstream, especially in deeper water. In this case the drift begins with the rod tip well down and the rod is then lifted while the line is being stripped in more quickly than the current, again causing the fly to rise up through the water.

THE CAREY SPECIAL

Leisenring and Hidy were by no means the only anglers creating soft-hackle patterns in the 1930s. One of the most effective and long-lasting flies from that era is the Carey Special that came from the vice of Colonel Thomas Carey in British Columbia, Canada. In one version of the history he was asked by Doctor Lloyd Day of Kelowna to tie a fly using hair from a marmot that the doctor had 'found'. In another version, the good Colonel, obsessed by a desire to tie the ideal lake trout fly, disappeared for several days and was found by a search party beside Arthur Lake, between Vernon and Kamloops, surrounded by heaps of dead pheasants as he searched for the perfect hackle feather. Either way, the outcome was a fly with an extremely long soft hackle that represents a dragonfly nymph but also a caddis or mayfly nymph, as well as a leech. It remains an extremely popular lake fly in British Columbia, generally tied on a 3XL hook with a body of peacock herl, chenille or dubbing with a tail and hackle of pheasant rump feather (sometimes dyed olive green), the hackle extending well past the bend of the hook. There are many colour variations, mainly using black, green and red materials, and a burnt orange version with a dyed guinea-fowl hackle is popular with steelheaders.

With or without a tail, the Carey Special (originally called the Monkey-faced Louise!) is an excellent searching pattern for still waters.

Matuka Streamer

YEAR: c.1950   **FLY TYER:** Anon.   **LOCATION:** New Zealand

The Original Recipe

Hook
6XL streamer hook, #1/0–#8

Wing
Two dyed hen back feathers

Thread
Black tying thread

Rib
Gold or silver wire or tinsel

Body
Black chenille

Hackle
Dyed hen hackle

Matuka is a style of tying that originated in New Zealand in the mid twentieth century and has since spread to Europe and the USA. It is an extremely effective way of creating a sinuous streamer of any size that moves realistically in the water to represent any number of baitfish.

Rainbow trout were introduced to New Zealand towards the end of the 19th century and they thrived in rich lakes such as famous Lake Taupo. Throughout the early part of New Zealand's fly fishing history anglers primarily used English-style trout flies, but when it came to simulating the plentiful indigenous baitfish something different was required. The coloration of the kaoro, a small mottled fish on which the trout feed, was found to be very similar to that of the feathers of the brown bittern, or 'matuku' in the Maori language, unfortunately for the bittern. The use of their feathers was finally banned to avoid them becoming extinct.

HALF-STRIPPED FEATHERS

The defining feature of the matuka streamer is a pair of feathers with the barbs removed from part of each quill so that the front portions sit directly on the hook with the full parts of the feathers forming a tail. Once the two feathers are in position, they are bound to the hook using the ribbing, which passes between the barbs of the feathers. The result is a fly that has an enticing action in the water and that avoids the problem common to many streamers of having the tail wrap around the bend of the hook when casting.

The matuka reached the USA in 1975 when Swisher and Richards wrote about it in *Fly Fishing Strategy*, describing it as their favourite streamer and recommending that it be tied with at least three pairs of wide hackle feathers. Once tied only in muted colours and cast for trout, some matukas today vie with the gaudiest of salmon flies and are used to fish for bass, sea trout and steelhead.

New Zealand's rainbow trout were the original target of the Matuka Streamer, but this elegant style of fly has since been successfully cast to a range of predatory fish.

Sol Duc Spey

YEAR: 1950s   **FLY TYER:** Syd Glasso   **LOCATION:** Forks, Washington State, USA

The **Original Recipe**

Hook
Up-eye salmon hook, #2–#1/0

Thread
Black tying thread

Tag
Flat silver tinsel

Body
Rear 2/3 – hot orange floss;
front 1/3 – hot orange goat dubbing

Rib
Oval silver tinsel

Body hackle
Yellow saddle hackle, long
and webby

Throat
Black heron substitute

Wing
Four hot orange hackle tips

When Syd Glasso began tying his first steelhead versions of
Spey flies in the late 1950s, he gave birth to an entirely new family
of flies, one that still thrives more than half a century later. Glasso's
attention to detail and careful selection of just the right materials
made his flies outstanding works of art. While the Spey form is still
evident (see the Lady Caroline, page 46), the Steelhead Speys are
sleeker, more sparsely tied, and, above all, more brightly coloured
than any traditional Scottish fly ever dreamed of becoming.

SPECIFICALLY PACIFIC

Syd Glasso was a schoolteacher in the small town of Forks on the Olympic
Peninsula in Washington State, virtually within casting distance of some
of the finest steelhead rivers in the Pacific Northwest. As well as being
a keen and accomplished steelheader, he was an expert Spey fly tyer (a
classic Spey fly tied by Glasso recently went on sale for $1,500!), and he
took what seemed to him a natural step – offering a version of the Scottish
Spey fly, designed to entice the Atlantic salmon, to its Pacific cousin.

*Found in Pacific-bound
rivers from southern
California to Alaska, the
steelhead is a sea-run
rainbow trout that returns
to fresh water to spawn.
Unlike Pacific salmon, the
majority of steelhead go back
to the ocean after spawning
and return repeatedly.*

Up until the mid 1950s, wet-fly steelhead anglers in this area had been using bucktail, hairwing and spider patterns, but here was something new. Unlike the true Spey fly, the Sol Duc Spey – named after Syd's local river – was slim and bright, with an orange body, yellow body hackles, a red head and four flaming orange hackle tips tied in a tented formation on top of the hook for wings.

Visibility was key, but the racy body style allowed the fly to sink quickly down to the fish, unlike its fatter forebears, and the exposed hook acted like a keel to hold the fly upright in the current.

CATCHING ON

It was a killer. Fishing the Sol Duc River, Glasso caught five steelhead the first time he used his new fly, and soon a small group of his friends were using this and several other classic Glasso patterns, most of them based on Spey fly principles. It didn't take long for further evolution to take place in the hands of such renowned tyers as Dick Wentworth, Pat Crane, and Walt Johnson, but it took a good many years before the Steelhead Speys found favour with a much wider audience. Now they are to be found catching fish throughout the Pacific Northwest, from Oregon to the famous rivers of northern British Columbia – such as the Skeena, Bulkley, Maurice and Babine – and Syd Glasso's influence is undoubtedly behind the popularity of fly tying on the West Coast over the last 30 years.

The Sol Duc River, which flows from the Olympic Mountains in Washington State, offers ideal conditions for the steelhead and a challenge for the angler in pursuit of the 'fish of a thousand casts'.

In an article entitled 'The Olympic Peninsula', published in *The Creel* magazine in 1970, Glasso wrote, 'I like Spey type flies for winter steelheading and have used them for over twenty years. The style is over a century old, they're easy to tie and they look seductive in the water. The fish take them solidly and that's enough for me.' Many would argue that they are far from easy to tie well, but fish certainly take them solidly.

Two-Feather Fly

YEAR: 1950   **FLY TYER:** Harry Darbee   **LOCATION:** New York State, USA

The Original Recipe

Hook
Short shank dry fly, up eye,
#10–#14

Thread
Black or white tying thread

Tail
Duck breast or flank feather,
tip removed

Body
Middle portion of same feather,
fibres pulled forwards

Wing
Bottom portion of same feather

Hackle
Dry fly hackle of choice

Harry Darbee and his wife Elsie are among the most celebrated of American fly tyers, renowned for their contributions to the Catskill tradition. Harry was also an entomologist and a fierce advocate for fish habitat protection. He is credited with the creation of several flies, but the Two-Feather is remarkable for its delicacy and innovative tying method.

MEETING THE CHALLENGE

As Harry Darbee told it in his book *Catskill Flytier: My life, times, and techniques*, published in 1977, he created the Two-Feather Fly in response to a request by the legendary fly fisher Terrell Moore. Artificials representing the larger mayflies, such as *Isonychia*, were tied on larger hooks and tended to be fairly heavy and bulky. They were difficult to present delicately, and Moore wanted a mayfly pattern for rivers and streams that weighed no more than the natural and that would land lightly on slow, clear, glassy water without spooking the fish. Darbee's unique solution was literally feather-light, composed of a single feather to create the tail, extended body and wings, and another for the hackle, tied on a short-shank, light-wire dry fly hook.

The finely barred flank feathers of the mallard are ideal for this pattern, providing the wings with a vague translucence and the body with a hint of segmentation.

THE TYING METHOD

The key to the 'Darbee', as it became known, is in the clever way the first feather is tied in. Taking the flank feather of a mallard, teal or wood duck (the correct size is critical), Harry snipped out the centre of the feather tip and then separated two fibres from each side to form the tail. The rest of the fibres were then stroked down the feather towards the stem to form a long, slim body that was then tied onto the hook shank so that the tail and body – the simplest detached body ever conceived – curved upwards and away from the hook. The remaining feather fibres formed the wings and a stiff hackle was then wound behind and in front of them. The resultant fly was light, graceful and buoyant, parachuting delicately on to the water the right way up and producing a very lifelike silhouette from below. For all its delicacy, the fly proved remarkably durable, probably because there is next to nothing for the trout to sink its teeth into.

The Two-Feather Fly became quite well known over the next few years and even appeared in an article by A.J. McLane in *Field & Stream* in 1960, but its popularity was short lived. Harry described it as 'too much of a novelty to last', and it disappeared from the mainstream.

Nonetheless, there were tyers and anglers who kept the method alive, including Dick Alf of Idaho who popularised what has now become known as the Hatchmaster or Hatchmaker method of tying. This Darbee-style fly is now being tied using a range of different feathers and in a spectrum of colours and sizes, since it can be tied to match a variety of hatches. The hackle can also be tied parachute style to settle the fly deeper into the surface layer. Some versions use a single feather for the tail and body but have wings added separately.

Harry and Elsie Darbee

Harry Darbee was born in the Catskills in 1906 and started his first professional fly tying business in partnership with Walt Dette in Roscoe in 1927. The enterprise was short lived, but the two of them, together with Walt's wife Winnie, set up shop again in the early 1930s with more success. They found themselves so busy that they hired someone to sort the hackles, a young woman from Neversink by the name of Elsie Bivins. She and Harry soon became romantically involved, married and set up their own fly tying business, specialising in dry flies in the style of such greats as Theodore Gordon. They became experts and, despite the Great Depression, their venture prospered.

While almost all tyers were using even-numbered hook sizes, Harry chose to go for the odd sizes – #15, #13, #11 etc. – which made his

"I began commercial fly tying because fishing seemed to be the only business that wasn't too affected by the depression."

Harry Darbee

flies subtly different from the majority. Besides the Catskill-style flies, he and Elsie gained a reputation for their spun deer hair flies, such as the Beaverkill Bastard, and for the quality of the hackles that they used. The Darbees refused to use dyed feathers, and Harry bred his own dun roosters to achieve precisely the shades he wanted. Together, Harry and Elsie became an institution, and their fly shop became a virtual clubhouse for the diverse characters who were fishing in the Catskills.

Elk Hair Caddis

YEAR: 1957   **FLY TYER:** Al Troth   **LOCATION:** Pennsylvania, USA

The Original Recipe

Hook
Dry fly, #12 – #18

Thread
Black, brown or tan
tying thread

Body
Dubbed fur or synthetic
dubbing

Palmered hackle
Deep red or ginger cock hackle

Rib
Gold wire counter wound

Head and Wing
Natural elk hair

Like another elk hair pattern, the Humpy, this fly, athough it was created in Pennsylvania, made its mark in the western United States, this time in south-western Montana. Whereas the Humpy simulates a great many things fairly well, the Elk Hair Caddis does just what it says on the box, and it does it so well that it has become a worldwide standard pattern.

FLOATING HIGH

In 1957, Al Troth set out to design a fairly buoyant emerging caddis pattern to fish the Loyalsock Creek, a tributary of the Susquehanna River, in Pennsylvania. What he actually created was a high floating pattern that mimicked a fluttering or spent adult green caddis. It is said that Troth took his inspiration from one of G.E.M. Skues's flies. Skues, although he is associated with the birth of true nymph fishing, created many realistic and highly effective dry fly patterns, and one of these was the Little Red Sedge. Here is Skues's own recipe, taken from *The Way of a Trout With a Fly*, published in 1921.

Replace the landrail feather with elk hair to form the tent-like wing and you have a very fine caddis pattern that floats so well it has no need of a front hackle — and that's just what Al Troth did. The fly didn't become well known until he published the details in an article in *The Fly Tyer Quarterly* in 1978, when it quickly found favour on the Yellowstone and Madison Rivers, and then throughout the continent and beyond for fast-flowing and pocket waters.

The Elk Hair Caddis is not only buoyant with a convincing silhouette but it also gives an impression of movement through the palmered hackle fibres that

Little Red Sedge

Hook: #1 down-eyed, square bend

Tying silk: Hot orange waxed with brown wax

Body hackle: Long, deep red cock, with short fibres, tied in at shoulder and carried down to tail

Rib: Fine gold wire, binding down body hackle

Body: Darkest hare's ear

Wings: Landrail wing, bunched and rolled, and tied on sloping well back over the tail

Front hackle: Like body hackle, but larger, and long enough to tie five or six turns in front of wing

keep it fluttering above the surface and the indistinct profile of the hair wing that looks as though it's in motion. For trout in rivers and on still waters it is generally tied in sizes from #10 down to #16, and on streams some anglers fish it as a duo fly, supporting a nymph through eddies and runs. In larger sizes, up to a #6, it can be fished for steelhead, too.

VARIATIONS

The best elk hair comes from the cow elk late in the season. The hair is long, pale, firm and extremely buoyant, as each hair contains tiny pockets of air.

The principal areas of change are the coloration of the elk hair (varying from bleached white through to dark brown and even black, as well as dyed options, especially olive green) and the dubbed body, which can be matched to the colour of the hair wing or changed to red, orange or yellow. For steelhead, the body dubbing is sometimes replaced with braid, floss or foam, and flash can be added.

The Peacock Caddis, a simplified version in which the dubbed body, hackle and gold wire rib are replaced with dark peacock herl, provides a good imitation of darker hatching caddis. This pattern sits lower in the water, which is an advantage on smooth water, and it can be tied on hooks as small as a #20 to serve as a midge pattern.

GODDARD CADDIS

The Goddard Caddis takes advantage of the fact that once it has been spun to form a dense matrix, elk hair can be sculpted very precisely with a sharp blade.

British fly tyers John Goddard and Clive Henry came up with a deer-hair caddis pattern in the early 1960s that is, if anything, even more buoyant than the Elk Hair Caddis. Several clumps of deer hair – between two and four, depending on the hook size – are spun around the back half of the bare hook shank and are then clipped or shaved into the characteristic caddis-wing tent shape. Once a pair of stripped neck hackle quills are tied in for antennae, a brown neck hackle is wound to form the front half of the fly. The antennae balance the fly as well as adding realism.

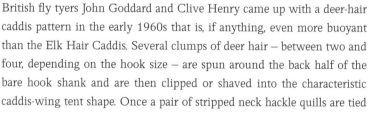

Goddard and Henry had enormous success with the G&H Sedge on lakes and reservoirs, drifting it with the breeze or skating it across the surface, and it proved equally effective on rivers, generally tied in smaller sizes.

Al Troth

The creator of the Elk Hair Caddis was a supremely practical man. Having spent some time in the Navy and as a metallurgist with Pittsburgh Steel, he attended teacher training college and then taught industrial arts for 15 years in Williamsport, Pennsylvania. He was able to turn his hand to anything, and taught everything from metal- and woodworking to small engines and drafting. Living close to Loyalsock Creek, he became an enthusiastic angler and fly tyer, as well as a keen photographer, making himself a waterproof Plexiglas box in order to photograph fish underwater.

He and his family spent many summers fishing in Montana, and in 1973 they moved to Dillon, MT, where Al started his own business as a fly tyer and fishing guide on the rivers of south-western Montana – rivers such as the Beaverhead and Big Hole, on which his

water-repellent fly showed its true worth. He began selling the pattern at Bud Lilly's Fly Shop in West Yellowstone and it was an instant success. The Elk Hair Caddis has since been featured three times on the cover of *Fly Fisherman* magazine, and Al himself has been the subject of many articles and has appeared in many books, as has his wildlife photography. Using his skills as both a fly tyer and a teacher, Al Troth wrote instructional articles on fly tying and contributed to many books. He also created his own version of Frank Sawyer's Pheasant Tail Nymph, using peacock herl as the thorax material.

In 1996 Al was forced by ill health to give up guiding. He died in 2012, but has left an indelible mark on fly fishing through the many people that he taught and guided personally, through his writing and photography and through a fly with which his name will always be associated.

It wasn't until the early 1970s that the fly made its debut in the USA, after Goddard and Henry gave the fly to Andre Puyans, a West Coast commercial fly tyer who had been a great advocate of the Humpy, and he marketed it as the Goddard Caddis. In North America it now has a great reputation on fast, rough water, floating like a cork and offering great visibility – to fish as well as fishers.

Lefty's Deceiver

YEAR: Late 1950s   **FLY TYER:** Lefty Kreh   **LOCATION:** Maryland, USA

The Original Recipe

Hook
Saltwater streamer, #2–#3/0

Body (optional)
Silver or pearl braid

Thread
Fairly heavy tying thread

Flanks / Belly
Two slim bundles of bucktail

Tail
Four to eight saddle feathers
and Krystal Flash

Back
Bucktail, darker than underside

During the 1940s fly casting for saltwater fish started to take off, using feathered streamers that followed the style of the New England tyers such as Carrie Stevens. One of the casters was Lefty Kreh, and in the late 1950s he set about solving a problem with the streamers, namely that in larger sizes the wet feather wings would foul up around the hook on the back cast. The flies also had a lot of wind resistance. The solution that he came up with – Lefty's Deceiver – has become one of the most popular streamers worldwide, in saltwater and fresh.

PROBLEM SOLVING

Lefty set very clear goals for his fly: won't foul the hook; looks like a fish and swims well; can be tied in any length and colour; cuts through the air and casts easily. To achieve these goals he chose to combine the sinuous qualities of a feather tail with the stiffness of a bucktail body, tying four to eight wide saddle hackles in at the bend of the hook and three slim bunches of bucktail in at the head extending beyond the bend of the hook, one each side and one – usually darker – on top of the shank.

'…a correctly tied Lefty's Deceiver lifted from the water for the back cast will travel through the air like a sleek knife blade'. **Left Kreh, Lefty Kreh's Ultimate Guide to Fly Fishing (2003)**

A seasoned speaker and demonstrator, Lefty has shared his knowledge of casting, fishing and fly tying across North America and, through the many books he has written, around the world.

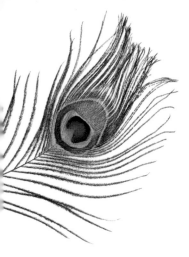

RAINBOW OFFSPRING

His design, initially tied in white, has spawned an entire family of flies in a wide variety of colours, a range of sizes, with the addition of peacock herl or various reflective synthetic materials, and with or without stick-on eyes, an epoxy head and a weed guard.

The flexibility of this pattern means that it can be adapted to match almost any bait fish. Lefty Kreh was originally targeting striped bass in the Chesapeake Bay, but there are few saltwater species that won't go for an appropriately tied Deceiver, as Lefty himself discovered in the waters around Florida. This pattern is now used for, among others, bluefish, sea trout, snook, tarpon and bonefish.

In fresh waters, too, this lifelike steamer has proved effective, being cast for trout, bass, pike and Amazonian golden dorado and peacock bass.

Peacock herl has become an important element in many saltwater flies, adding sinuous iridescence to bucktail and other patterns.

LEFTY'S COMPOSITE CAST

Also known by anglers as Choppers and Slammers, and with good reason, bluefish are a favourite for saltwater fly anglers. The Deceiver is a favourite for bluefish, which commonly reach 20lb (9kg). Just avoid their teeth.

Lefty's ambition of creating a fly that would cast into the wind didn't stop there. A keen freshwater fly angler and an expert caster, he recognised that the traditional casting method of holding the rod up and using the forearm to move it back and forth between the 10 o'clock and 2 o'clock positions has its limitations when it comes to saltwater casting. The technique is fine for light flies on small rivers, but keeping the line high above the water means it catches more wind, and the short stroke makes it harder to impart the necessary power to a heavier fly over long distances. So, never averse to courting controversy, Lefty set about developing his own style of casting.

The cast begins with about 20ft (6m) of line on the water, the rod tip about a foot off the water, and no slack line. The rod is raised quickly to lift the line off the water and the wrist is then snapped back to bring the rod up and back, pointing slightly away from the body. Once the rod is about 15 degrees past the vertical you stop applying power but – and here is the big difference – you allow your arm to continue drifting back until is the rod almost horizontal as the line straightens

Lefty Kreh

Tutored in his early 20s by Joe Brooks, the popular fly fishing writer and one of the pioneers of adventure fly fishing in remote locations (and a fellow resident of Maryland), Lefty was encouraged to take up writing too and landed a job with the *Frederick News-Post* in the early 1950s. He soon gained a reputation for his readable and informative style, and within a few years he was writing for 11 newspapers. Spending much of his time fishing with Joe, especially around the Chesapeake Bay, it was during this period that he developed the Deceiver and did so much to promote saltwater fly fishing, which was very much a minority sport at the time.

Lefty spent most of the 1960s living in South Florida, and there he organised the Miami Metropolitan Fishing Tournament, the world's most prestigious fishing tournament at the time, as well as writing for the *Miami Herald* and co-founding the *Florida Sportsman* magazine. Returning to Maryland in the early 1970s, he

spent the next 20 years as outdoor editor for the *Baltimore Sun*, but his interests continued to expand to encompass photography, public speaking, fly-casting demonstrations, television appearances, writing for magazines, and extending the range of the sport by fly fishing for species that most people thought impossible, such as tarpon and tuna. In the course of his career Lefty has fished in many parts of the world, from Iceland to the South Pacific, and he has shared the wealth of his experience by writing more than 20 books, one of his most influential being *Fly Fishing in Salt Water*, published in 1974.

Lefty's contributions to the sport and to conservation have been recognised by a host of awards, including the American Sportfishing Association's Lifetime Achievement Award and induction into the Freshwater Fishing Hall of Fame, the Fly Fishing Hall of Fame and the IGFA Hall of Fame.

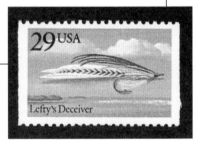

out. As Lefty wrote in what he calls his 'blasphemous article' in *Outdoor Life* in 1965, 'At the completion of your back cast, you should be able to look over your shoulder, through the guides and down your line.'

In the forward cast the hand comes down to shoulder height and moves through horizontally, bringing the rod forwards and then driving the rod down until the rod tip is pointing a few feet above the target as the line unfurls. Unconventional it may be, but saltwater anglers the world over can attest to it being effective.

Lefty's Deceiver was one of five flies honoured by the US Mail in 1991. The set of 29c stamps included the Royal Wulff and the Muddler Minnow.

Pheasant Tail Nymph

YEAR: 1958   **FLY TYER:** Frank Sawyer   **LOCATION:** Wiltshire, England

The Original Recipe

Hook
Wet fly, #10–#16

Thread
Fine copper wire (on ceramic bobbin)

Tail
Cock pheasant tail fibres

Body
Cock pheasant tail fibres

Rib (and underbody)
Fine copper wire

Wing case
Cock pheasant tail fibres

Some flies just have it: that indefinable essential quality, some combination of form, texture, colour and action that just hits the spot. Frank Sawyer certainly found it when he created the Pheasant Tail Nymph, but it wasn't by accident. A river keeper on the famous Hampshire Avon for half a century and more, he spent most of his life not only fishing but studying the trout and the invertebrates on which they fed, and his efforts paid off. Sawyer's Pheasant Tail Nymph now has a worldwide reputation and has caught more trout around the world and sired more variations than virtually any other fly.

SOURCES OF INSPIRATION

The Hampshire Avon, which rises in the north of Wiltshire and makes its meandering way some 60 miles (96km) southwards to the coast at Christchurch, is reputed to have the greatest diversity of life forms of any river in Britain, and is especially rich in mayflies. Frank Sawyer tied the Pheasant Tail to give an impression of a drifting and emerging *Baetis*, or olive, nymph, with its small head, rounded thorax, thin tapering abdomen and relatively short tail. The PTN emulates these physical characteristics with admirable simplicity and fools fish on chalk and freestone streams as well as on still waters. Sawyer gained some inspiration for his fly from a much older pattern, the Pheasant Tail Red Spinner, a dry fly that Sawyer had noted would still take fish once it had become submerged.

It is clear from the colour and form of this Baetis *nymph why the PTN would be mistaken for one, but it is less clear why one of the world's best-known flies works so well in so many locations and under such a wide range of conditions.*

Nowadays you'll find many suggested ways of tying the basic fly, but Sawyer's was the most minimalist, using only a small bunch of ringneck pheasant centre tail-feather fibres to form the tail, abdomen, thorax and wing case, and fine copper wire to tie them in, provide the ribbing and add a little weight in the form of a wire ball thorax, as well as giving the nymph a little sparkle.

G.E.M. Skues had earlier created a soft hackle nymph that had a pheasant tail body, but Sawyer, who was a keen observer, had noticed that the vulnerable nymphs kept their legs close in to their bodies when they were swimming, and he therefore created a slim, streamlined fly with no legs. This allowed it to enter the water with little splash and to sink quickly down to the required depth, aided by the weight of the wire.

'General shape and colouration, together with the right size, is of greater importance than an exact copy. My two universal patterns, as I call them, are the Pheasant Tail and the Grey Goose. The Pheasant Tail serves for the darker coloured nymphs and the Gray Goose for the lighter ones.' **Frank Sawyer, *Nymphing in the Classic Style*, in *The Masters on the Nymph* (1979)**

THE INDUCED TAKE

Sawyer's quick-sinking fly is in marked contrast to the much lighter hackled nymphs of G.E.M. Skues, and the method of fishing it is equally different. Although the PTN can be fished in the surface layers, its home is in the deeper water, and to take full advantage of its properties Sawyer developed a technique, known as the induced take, that continues to prove effective with a wide range of nymph patterns.

The induced take is designed to be used on clear rivers with steady current and moderate depth, fishing to targeted trout or grayling that are 'nymphing' – moving from side to side and opening their mouths as they take nymphs that are being brought to them in the current. The angler is positioned upstream and across from the fish and the fly is cast upstream so that the fly, on a dead drift with the rod tip following the fly, has sunk

to the level of the fish by the time it enters the fish's field of vision. Sawyer was aware that fish holding in a feeding lane are faced with a steady flow of not only food but also general bits of vegetation and detritus, and that an artificial nymph on a perfect dead drift stands a good chance of being ignored. The secret of the induced take is to bring the fly to the trout's attention by stopping the rod and raising the tip slightly, causing the fly to swing upwards in the current in front of the fish, like a swimming nymph that is about to get away. Watch for the fish to follow and, when you see the tell-tale white of the open jaws or you calculate that the fish has taken the nymph, raise the rod tip to set the hook, but you may not have to, as induced takes can be aggressive.

Sawyer's 'induced take' method of fishing his fast-sinking nymphs works equally well for trout and for the grayling, 'the lady of the stream'.

VARIATIONS ON THE PTN

The first person to experiment with different versions of the Pheasant Tail was Sawyer himself, not only tying the fly in a wide range of sizes – it is a pattern that lends itself to being tied in any size from a #10 to a #22 – but also changing the colour completely by using goose feather fibres. The Grey Goose simulates lighter coloured nymphs, such as the Pale Watery, and can be fished in the same way as the PTN. Sawyer maintained that with these two nymphs in various sizes he could represent virtually all the nymphs of the Avon, and he rarely fished any other nymph patterns.

Sawyer generally tied the fly on a standard length hook, but the late and well-respected Arthur Cove created

Using the same tying method with Grey Goose feather fibres, Sawyer created the pale nymph version.

his own version by tying the nymph without a tail on a long-shank hook, wrapping further around the bend of the hook and giving it a fuller thorax of rabbit fur. With a profile more like that of a sedge or overgrown chironomid pupa, Cove's Pheasant Tail proved to be remarkably effective on the trout reservoirs of the English Midlands.

In America, with its own spectrum of mayflies, the tendency has been to tie this pattern on longer hooks and also to do away with the wire ball thorax, using the copper wire solely for ribbing and tying the fly with thread. Some tyers have also added legs to the pattern, and Al Troth (see Elk Hair Caddis, page 136) also gave the fly a lead wire wrap and a peacock herl thorax to create what has become known as the American Pheasant Tail. Endless further variations include bead heads, hackles, crystal flash, hare's ear thorax, flashbacks, fluorescent hotspots and the use of dyed pheasant tail feathers in olive or yellow olive. In different sizes and colours, the PTN has stood in for just about everything from a midge pupa to the largest stonefly nymph, all of which just goes to show the versatility of Sawyer's simply tied and impressionistic fly.

Frank Sawyer

Born in the village of Bulford, beside the Avon in Wiltshire, England, Frank Sawyer was given the job of assistant keeper on a stretch of that river at the age of 19. Three years later, in 1928, he became head keeper for what was to become the Services Dry Fly Fishing Association, a fly fishing club for the Armed Forces at Netheravon. He was to hold that position for more than 50 years, during which time he became, quite literally, world famous. Mentored by members of the Association, he met G.E.M. Skues and other influential men who admired his powers of observation and the depth of his knowledge and who enabled him to broaden his horizons.

In the course of his long career he wrote magazine articles and then books, went on fishing trips across Europe and finally became a broadcaster for BBC radio and television. His books *Keeper of the Stream* (1952) and *Nymphs and the Trout* (1958), in which he first described the Pheasant Tail Nymph, were highly acclaimed, and in 1979 he was awarded the MBE (Member of the British Empire) for his contribution to fishing and conservation. Frank Sawyer died the following year on the banks of his beloved river.

Al Troth's version of the Pheasant Tail Nymph, with its peacock herl thorax and pheasant tail fibre legs, now competes with the original in popularity, especially in the USA. There are now literally dozens of variations on Sawyer's original theme.

NETHERAVON STYLE

Sawyer's style of fishing, which became known as the Netheravon school, had as much of an ethical code as chalk stream dry fly angling. Its principles, similar to those practised by G.E.M. Skues, were laid out by Oliver Kite, Sawyer's angling colleague and a fellow resident of Netheravon, whose own books and TV series introduced a wide audience to Sawyer's fishing style:

- No flies on hooks larger than a #14.
- No use of nymphs during a mayfly hatch (dry fly only at that time).
- Only cast upstream or up and across.
- Only cast to trout that are likely to be feeding on nymphs.
- Only cast to fish that have been located.

This last edict included the possibility of casting to fish that could realistically be predicted to be in a particular location, but forbade flogging the whole river in the hope of finding a fish. Dry fly traditionalists accused the nymph anglers of doing precisely that and considered it unworthy of the sport.

Sawyer has often been cited as the successor to G.E.M. Skues. He had a huge impact on the development of nymph fishing and did so with the active support and encouragement of the great man. The great difference between them was that Sawyer, effectively the originator of weighted nymphs, took this form of fishing to new depths.

The River Avon (seen here at Bulford, the village where he was born) provided a rich and rewarding focus for the whole of Frank Sawyer's life.

'When I first started to write about nymph-fishing, soon after the Second World War, I had no idea that the time might arrive when nymphs would become so popular and likely to supersede the conventional wet-flies as a means of taking fish in most of our waters about the country. Nor do I think G.E.M. Skues had this in mind, for no longer can nymph-fishing be described as "Minor Tactics".'
Frank Sawyer, quoted in *Frank Sawyer's Nymphing Secrets*, by Nick Sawyer

Dave's Hopper

YEAR: 1959   **FLY TYER:** Dave Whitlock   **LOCATION:** Oklahoma, USA

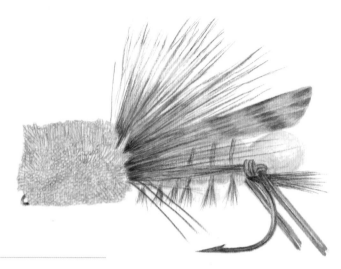

The Original Recipe

Hook
3XL, 2X heavy wire, #6–#12

Thread
Yellow tying thread

Tail
Coarse red deer hair

Body
Yellow polypropylene yarn

Hackle
Grizzly brown

Wing
Mottled brown turkey quill over
yellow-dyed deer hair

Legs
Ringneck pheasant tail fibres,
knotted

Collar and head
Natural deer hair

Flies with heads of spun deer hair have been around since the early 20th century and, as we have seen, came into common usage with Don Gapen's Muddler Minnow and the many offspring that it sired, but Dave Whitlock of Oklahoma took the concept in a new direction in the mid 1950s when he applied it to a hopper pattern.

Grasshoppers are at their most plentiful at the height of summer, when hatches of aquatic insects tend to be sporadic, so when young hoppers land on the water on hot and windy days, the trout are often happy to eat them. Live hoppers have long been used as bait, and there have been many hopper-like patterns over the centuries. One of the most realistic of these is the Michigan Hopper developed by Art Winnie of Traverse City, Michigan, in the early 1940s. A barber and commercial fly tyer, he is reputed to have tied more than 200,000 flies in the course of his career. The fly was popularised by Joe Brooks (a great advocate of the Muddler Minnow) in the 1950s and became known as Joe's Hopper, and this is the pattern that Dave Whitlock adapted to the Muddler style.

If there is one quality that Joe's Hopper could do with more of, it is buoyancy, and it is frequently (and effectively) fished subsurface, although some modern versions now feature a foam body. Dave kept many of the original fly's attributes, including the yarn body (replacing wool with poly yarn), the red bucktail tail and the turkey feather wings, but he increased the buoyancy by adding a Muddler-type spun deer hair head and collar, trimming the head to an exaggerated square shape. He also added very realistic legs made by knotting small bunches of feather fibres, a process that requires a little practice and, ideally, the right tool for the job. Dave's Hopper has since become a classic and is one of the most popular grasshopper patterns ever.

It is generally fished, on still or moving water, close to the bank – or even bounced off it – with a none-too-gentle presentation, left to sit and then stripped in short jerks to

Grasshoppers provide fish with an attractive food item when winged adults and clumsy youngsters fall onto the water's surface at the hottest times of the year.

simulate the struggling terrestrial. When trout are already turned on to hoppers they will travel some distance to take this one. Casting further out can also be successful when winged adults are taking to the air.

PARALLEL EVOLUTION

Away to the east, in Pennsylvania, another fly tyer had a similar idea independently. Ed Shenk came up with his legless Letort Hopper towards the end of the 1950s, a smaller and slimmer fly, generally tied in sizes #10 to #16, with a yellow dubbing body, turkey slip wings and a trimmed square deer hair head and hackle. It, too, remains a popular pattern.

Meanwhile, the Muddler was making inroads in Australia. In 1962, fly tyer Dušan (Dan) Todorivic was fly fishing on the Murrumbidgee River, in New South Wales, where bait fishing with natural grasshoppers was big but the hopper patterns he was using were proving ineffective. Loathe to resort to bait fishing, Dan tied up a new imitation using yellow chenille for the body and golden pheasant tippet for underwings (grasshoppers use their bright underwings for amorous communication). For the two long hind legs he tied in trimmed dyed red hackle stems parallel to the hook shank, and the wings and head/hackle were what he had been using to tie Muddlers: mottled turkey feather and deer hair. With its long body and bulbous head, it didn't take long for Dan's Hopper to become the Nobby Hopper, and so it remains.

At his home in Oklahoma, Dave works on a fruit-cocktail-coloured Whit Hairbug, one of the great many flies he has invented.

A smaller version – Noel's Nobby Hopper – was created by Noel Jetson in Tasmania, where the grasshoppers are smaller than on the Australian continent, and a similar process occurred in South Africa, where the red legs gained a knotted joint in the same way as Dave's Hopper.

THE PROLIFIC TYER

Dave Whitlock has rightly been credited with creating more original flies than almost any other current tyer, and several of these make excellent use of deer hair.

Mouse patterns for large bass, pike and muskies date back at least a hundred years, and some of these were made of deer hair, but Dave Whitlock's

Mouse Rat has set the standard for the modern mouse fly. A far cry from a delicate mayfly, this deer hair mouse with its black, beady eyes and leather ears and tail is used in Alaska and Russia for steelhead and salmon, and on the roaring rivers of Mongolia for the magnificent taimen, a landlocked member of the salmon family that can reach 100lb (45kg).

In addition to a series of 'Red-Head' deer hair chugger bugs, Dave is responsible for the Matuka Sculpin, a Matuka-style streamer with a Muddler head and hackle on which he took his personal best brown trout, weighing over 22lb (10kg), as well as a 15lb (6.8kg) rainbow.

ANGLING DEVOTEE

Dave Whitlock gave up a career as a research chemist in 1970 in order to devote himself to his many fishing-related interests. Besides inventing and tying flies, he is a keen photographer, writer, conservationist and illustrator, and he has contributed images and text to countless magazines and books, including four of his own books.

He has also appeared in instructional videos and on television, he gives lectures and teaches fly fishing courses, and he has received several awards for wild trout propagation, conservation and fly tying. Dave is a recipient of the Fly Fishing Federation's Ambassador Award for national and international promotion of fly fishing and conservation.

In 2005, he and his wife Emily moved to Welling in eastern Oklahoma, where – among all their other activities – they run a fly shop. The town is in the foot-hills of the Ozark Mountains, an area famous for its trout-filled, spring-fed streams and rich lakes.

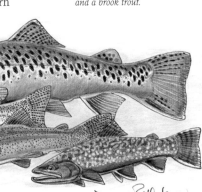

In his spare time(!) Dave is an accomplished illustrator. This painting, entitled 'Grand Slam', features a German brown, a rainbow, a Yellowstone cutthroat and a brook trout.

Comparadun

YEAR: 1974   **FLY TYER:** Al Caucci   **LOCATION:** Pennsylvania, USA

The Original Recipe

Hook
Dry fly, #12–#20

Wing
Natural coastal deer hair

Thread
Black tying thread

Body
Dry fly dubbing

Tail
Microfibetts, split

Head
Varnished tying thread

Since the introduction of the true dry fly, mayfly patterns have almost invariably incorporated a hackle – either as a collar or in parachute form – but there is also an illustrious line of hackle-free dries that dates back to the 1940s. Great advances were made in the late 1960s and the 1970s, including the introduction of the Comparadun, and in recent years the availability of highly buoyant tying materials has led to further new developments.

MESSY BUT EFFECTIVE

One of the oldest no-hackle dries is the Haystack, created by Fran Betters of the Adirondacks in 1949 when he was still a teenager. He later became a professional fly tyer and the founding owner of the Adirondack Sport Shop in the town of Wilmington, NY, close to the AuSable River, around which his life revolved. The AuSable Wulff is another of his inventions.

Fran Betters, seen here tying an AuSable Wulff at his bench, has been credited as one of the most inventive of fly tyers, putting his deep knowledge of the AuSable River to good use.

A far cry from the neat and tidy Quill Gordon, the Haystack is, as its name suggests, a scruffy and indeterminate pattern, but its combination of a splayed deer hair tail, deer hair wing tied well back from the eye, shaggy possum fur dubbing and hot orange head creates a buoyant fly that has proven irresistible to trout for decades.

The author of *Fran Betters' Fly Fishing, Fly Tying and Pattern Guide* (1986) also invented the Usual, another pattern designed to ride the tumbling waters of the AuSable but this time tied with fur from the feet of the snowshoe hare.

Fran was renowned for knowing his river intimately, drawing his own maps of the area and advising a constant stream of visitors to his shop on where, how and what fly to fish on the AuSable.

The tail played a vital role in Fran Betters' Haystack, giving it both buoyancy and stability, and the tail performs the same duty in the fly that Doug Swisher and Carl Richards introduced in their ground-breaking book *Selective Trout*, published in 1971. The book was the product of their intensive study of what trout actually see as a fly floats into view above them, and what cues cause the fish to take a fly. Using specially adapted cameras and microscopes they observed natural flies and fish behaviour in a range of rivers and in aquariums, and they concluded that the abdomen and the wing profile were far more important as triggers than the legs/hackle. This led them to develop several new fly patterns, the most important of which was the No-Hackle Dry Fly, tied on a 3XL fine wire hook with a split tail of dry fly hackle fibres, a dubbed fur body, and wings of duck primary wing quill or duck shoulder feather set low on the body so that the trailing edges rest on the surface of the water. Together with the tail, the wings give the fly stability and offer the fish a realistic silhouette of a newly emerged dun. It proved to be a deadly imitation, outfishing hackled dries in many situations, and the innovative work of Swisher and Richards brought hackle-free flies to the forefront. In 2011 the two men were inducted into the Fly Fishing Hall of Fame.

Vince Marinaro

The development of the hackle-free fly owes much to Vince Marinaro's thorax–style of dry fly tying in which the wing is set well back on the hook and the tail fibres are widely splayed. His flies do have hackles, but they are tied in such a way as to give the fish a clear view of the wing from below. Marinaro – another Flyfishing Hall of Fame inductee – was also something of a pioneer in the use of photography to study rises and the fish's view of the fly.

COMPARADUN

If there is a downside to the No-Hackle fly it is that the setting of the wings requires a good deal of skill, and that the wings themselves prove fragile when taken by a fish – which they will be. In 1975, Al Caucci and Bob Nastasi, in their book *Hatches: A Complete Guide to Fishing the Hatches of North American Trout Streams*, introduced a no-hackle style of fly that was, in many respects, a tidy and sparsely dressed descendant of Fran Betters' Haystack. It was called the Comparadun, not because of any connection with the parachute-hackled Paradun but following the theme of their earlier, widely acclaimed book *Compara-hatch*, published in 1973.

The Comparadun has an uplifted tail of hackle fibres or microfibetts, a thinly dubbed body and – the key to the pattern – a deer hair wing that forms a semi-circular fan across the top half of the fly. This gives it the appropriate silhouette, as well as stability and buoyancy, and the fly sits flush on the surface, making it suitable for slow-moving water. The form of the wing almost guarantees that the fly will land the right way up on

the water and will stay that way. Quick to construct and durable, the Comparadun can be tied in a range of colours and sizes to represent almost any adult mayfly, especially newly hatched or crippled duns.

A variation on the Comparadun, the Sparkle Dun, has a trailing poly yarn shuck that turns this pattern into a highly effective emerger. There are also versions of both flies that use synthetic materials in place of deer hair for the wing.

For their contributions to fly fishing, and for the five highly influential books that they co-authored, Bob Nastasi and Al Caucci were inducted into the Flyfishing Hall of Fame in 2006.

Al Caucci still has confidence in the fly he created some 40 years ago, and here he holds up a 20in (50cm) brown trout that took a #18 Pale Morning Dun Comparadun on the Beaverhead in Montana.

NEW MATERIALS

The availability of a wide variety of new synthetic fly tying materials has led tyers such as John R. Gantner of California to revisit the No-Hackle Dry Fly of Swisher and Richards and remedy some of its shortcomings while retaining its excellent fish-fooling qualities.

The use of materials such as cellophane, closed-cell foam, synthetic dry fly dubbing and monofilament has made it possible to design no-hackles that are much easier to tie than the originals, are more durable and more buoyant (making them suitable for more turbulent water), can be tied on heavier and stronger hooks, and that almost invariably sit the right way up on the water. The materials can be selected or hand coloured to match the natural insects.

Gantner exhorts anglers to return to the teachings of Swisher and Richards and to apply the modern materials, and he has created a range of 'Nu-No Hackle' flies to prove his point.

Booby Fly

YEAR: c.1975   **FLY TYER:** Gordon Fraser   **LOCATION:** Leicestershire, England

The Original Recipe

Hook
1XL nymph, #8–#12

Thread
Olive-green tying thread

Eyes
Expanded polystyrene balls
in nylon mesh

Tail
Olive marabou

Body
Olive chenille

Rib
Fine gold wire

Unlike the majority of flies in this book, most of which can trace the broad outlines of their ancestry back for several decades, if not centuries, the Booby fly has a remarkably short pedigree, owing its existence to the advent of a new material. It also stands out as possibly the only fly whose use raises ethical questions. Frederic Halford may have had issues with nymph patterns in general, but when this particular fly first hit the water he was probably turning in his grave.

In the 1970s, the British fly tyer and author Gordon Fraser, creator of the Fraser nymph, recognised the potential for a fly whose action and depth could be controlled not by its weight but by its buoyancy. In the previous decade, when expanded polystyrene was becoming commonplace, this lightweight material had already found a place in the fly tyer's arsenal. Fly fishers on the English lakes and reservoirs had observed that some emergers appear to rise through the water and hang in the surface film aided by a bubble of gas, and a small expanded polystyrene ball mimicked this perfectly, as well as representing the unfurling wings of an emerging fly or the gills of a chironomid pupa.

The white polystyrene balls that Fraser originally used have since been superseded by much tougher forms of closed cell foam that are available in a range of shapes and colours.

Fraser took this idea further and came up with the Booby fly, so called because…well, let's just say the fly has also been referred to as a Dolly Parton. Materials and tying methods have evolved since, but the bulbous bug eyes were originally tied using two small white expanded polystyrene balls trapped inside a piece of nylon tights and tied in behind the eyes using figure-of-eight wraps. The typical booby fly has a long marabou tail, which imparts a lot of motion to the fly, and a chenille body, but the range of possibilities is limitless.

Initially the Booby was worked on the surface using a dry line, like a floating Woolly Bugger, and they work well like this for bass, skated across the water. Trout, too, will go for this noisy surface action, but Fraser and others soon moved to a sinking line and opened up a world of new possibilities. On a slow-sinking intermediate line the fly can be fished at any depth and at any speed, and stripping the line produces an enticing action as the buoyant fly dives downwards following the curve of the line and then floats gently up. (On waters where multiple flies are allowed, the Booby can be fished on the top dropper with imitative patterns suspended below it, or on the point with other flies hanging from the horizontal leader – the aptly named washing-line method.)

The Booby fly can be tied to represent a damselfly larva, and retrieved to simulate its movement as it hovers and dives among the weed fronds on the lake bed.

With a full sinking line, the effect is even more spectacular. The line can be allowed to sink until it lies along the bed of the lake or reservoir, while the Booby, on a leader as short as 2ft (60cm), floats off the bottom, hovering above any weed that may be there. Short strips with long pauses will cause the fly to dive, rise and hang, giving a realistic impression of a dragonfly nymph or struggling bait fish, and when used in deep water in early spring, when the water is cold and the fish are down deep, this method can catch when little else will work. Using a loop knot to the hook allows the fly to dance on the rise and fall, making the most of the waving marabou tail, but a Booby will often be taken during the pause.

THE SINS OF THE STATIC FLY

Many kinds of fly are taken while hanging motionless in the water – chironomid pupa patterns are a good example – but the fly fisher generally knows all about it. Chironomids tend to be hit hard, and whether the leader is hanging directly down from the rod tip or is being fished on a floating line, with or without a strike indicator, there is no mistaking the fact that the fly has been taken.

With the Booby fly it's a very different story. When the angler is using the bottom-up method and the long sinking line is lying on the lake bed, unless the angler is in tight contact with the fly and is working it, a fish can chew on the fly without giving any indication until it turns away. The result can be a fatally deep-hooked fish. The Booby fly has been banned on some English waters partly because it is so effective, but also because of the risk the fly poses to fish in the hands of an unscrupulous angler. There have certainly been instances of anglers casting the fly out, putting the rod down and simply waiting, which is a long way from most people's idea of fly fishing, but even when fished carefully a Booby can be taken deeply, making it unpopular on catch-and-release fisheries. Boobies are generally tied on short hooks to reduce this problem.

MODERN VARIATIONS

Expanded polystyrene has largely been replaced by other types of closed-cell foam, especially polyethylene foams such as Ethafoam® and Plastazote®, as they are less prone to being flattened when chomped. Booby eyes are sold as pre-formed dumbbells or as cylinders of foam that can be cut to length, rounded off with scissors and tied onto a thread base a couple of eye-widths back from the eye. For the best of old and new, cut pieces of modern foam into small spheres and then tie them on trapped in a patch of nylon mesh to create even more durable 'eyes'.

Unlike the original polystyrene, modern foam is now available in a wide range of colours that can be used in creative ways, and while marabou tails remain, Booby bodies can be made of materials such as dubbing, peacock herl, rabbit fur strips and marabou. Booby flies first appeared in olive green and black, but gaudy is now the order of the day, with red, orange, bright yellow, chartreuse and plenty of sparkle becoming essential parts of the wardrobe, as well as palmered hackles, gold ribbing and stick-on eyes. These bright and bold flies are commonly used for large- and smallmouth bass (especially on the surface), perch, chub, carp, sea trout and steelhead, and even sea bass.

For these attractor patterns the term 'nymph' has largely been dropped, and quite rightly so, but at the same time there has been a trend towards tying booby versions of traditional nymph patterns such as the hare's ear, the diawl bach and even the pheasant tail, adding a foam head that allows these flies, too, to be fished 'bottom up' or hovering in midwater with extremely good results.

Until the early 20th century, marabou feathers came from the fine undertail coverts of the marabou stork, but this bird is now protected under CITES (the Convention on International Trade in Endangered Species). Fly tyers' marabou now comes from the back end of turkeys and chickens.

Crazy Charlie

YEAR: 1977   **FLY TYER:** Bob Nauheim   **LOCATION:** Bahamas

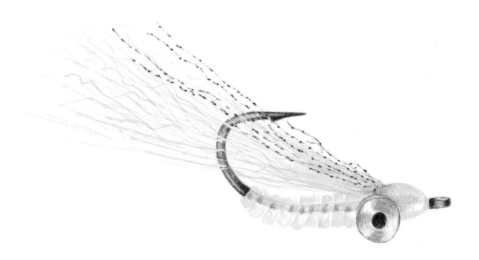

The Original Recipe

Hook
Saltwater, #2–#8

Thread
Yellow tying thread

Eyes
Bead chain or dumbbell eyes

Underbody
Pearlescent tinsel

Body
Clear vinyl V-rib (originally clear mono)

Wing
Calf hair and flash

The names by which it is known – grey ghost, torpedo of the flats, even its Latin name *Albula vulpes* (white fox) – reflect the awe in which the bonefish is held, considered pound for pound one of the hardest-fighting sport fish and certainly one of the fastest. In the 1970s, when relatively few people were fly fishing for these marvellous fish, Bob Nauheim came up with a fly that remains one of the most popular and that has fathered many of the modern bonefish patterns.

NASTY AND CRAZY

Bonefish are widely distributed in tropical waters around the globe, but for the fly fisherman it is the flats, where the water is shallow, food rich and warm, that provide the sport. In 1977, while fishing the flats in the Bahamas, Bob Nauheim saw bonefish feeding on glass minnows and was told by guide and lodge owner Charlie Smith that this was a common food item. That evening Bob tied some flies 'with a bit of flash, some clear 15lb (6.8kg) mono, a couple of feathers and a pair of bead eyes....It was the first time bead eyes were used on a bonefish pattern.' The following day the fly proved so successful that Charlie Smith referred to it as 'nasty', and Nasty Charlie it became. However, when it made its way into the Orvis catalogue it did so under the name of Crazy Charlie, and that is the name that stuck.

An angler on the flats off Aitutaki in the Cook Islands casts for bonefish. Growing up to 20lb (9kg), a bonefish can take line well into the backing in a matter of seconds.

THE MODERN PATTERN

With its underbody of pearl Flashabou wrapped with clear vinyl V-rib, calf tail wing, dumbbell eyes and upturned hook, the Crazy Charlie is generally fished on the bottom with a sink-and-draw retrieve, simulating a shrimp rather than a bait fish. The original fly was tied in white, but it is now found in a range of colours and sizes, with the eyes sized to suit the required sink rate. A version with a silver tinsel underbody and a wing of saddle hackle has retained the name of Nasty Charlie.

In bright and shallow conditions, where the flashiness of this fly might spook the fish, Martin Joergensen's Gotcha – with a tail of pearl, silver or gold Mylar® tubing, a body of Mylar braid and a wing of craft fur – offers a more subtle alternative. This fly is also good for permit.

Ally's Shrimp

YEAR: 1981   **FLY TYER:** Alastair Gowans   **LOCATION:** Perthshire, Scotland

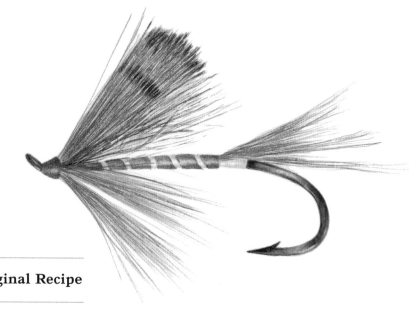

The **Original Recipe**

Hook
Salmon, #12–#4

Thread
Orange tying thread

Tag
Gold tinsel

Body
Orange floss and black floss

Rib
Gold tinsel

Belly / Underwing
Grey squirrel fur

Wing
Orange-dyed golden
pheasant tippet

Hackle
Orange-dyed hen hackle

While many traditional salmon flies, such as the Dee and Spey patterns, have shrimp- or prawn-like qualities, Ally's Shrimp comes from a line of more representational shrimp patterns, not just in looks but also in motion. Alastair Gowans' creation is now one of the most popular flies for Atlantic salmon in Ireland and Scotland, as well as across Europe and Russia, with a growing numbers of devotees on the salmon rivers of the east coast of North America, such as New Brunswick's Miramichi.

IRISH ORIGINS

Many species of shrimp and prawn form an essential element in the diet of the salmon while it's at sea, so it is entirely logical to present the fish with this staple when it reaches fresh water, arousing its predatory instinct. Indeed, natural prawn and shrimp bait fishing has a long tradition on the rivers of Scotland and Ireland, and is considered so effective that it is now generally banned for the sake of the stocks.

The first true shrimp pattern for salmon was tied in Ireland in the 1930s by Pat Curry of Coleraine, on the River Bann in County Londonderry. Curry's Red Shrimp has a tail of red golden pheasant breast feathers, as do most of the variations and alternative shrimp patterns that followed. These trailing fibres represent the shrimp's antennae.

Shrimps and prawns are an important food item, and many salmon and steelhead patterns for Pacific and Atlantic waters mimic their form and colour.

The General Practitioner, created by Lt Colonel Esmond Drury in 1953 for fishing English salmon rivers, was another milestone in shrimp flies, using the black stripes in golden pheasant tippets to represent the eyes, a trick that has been taken up by countless patterns since. This fly, which lacks the trailing fibres of Curry's pattern, is still popular, especially with steelheaders in the Pacific Northwest.

While aboard an Atlantic lobster trawler, Ally Gowans, a professional fly fisherman in the heart of the Scottish Highlands, noticed prawns that were 'long, slim and very active', had a noticeable black gut and were slightly orange in colour. In 1981 he captured this look using bucktail for the antennae, grey squirrel fur top and bottom, and adding a long-fibred collar hackle, all of which animate the fly as it moves through the water. Black floss on the front half of the hook shank simulates the gut, and golden pheasant tippet feathers play the part of the eyes and carapace.

The pattern is often tied on a double hook, but where such hooks are banned, such as in North America and the Kola Peninsula in Russia, it lends itself equally to a single. Ally's Shrimp can be tied in a wide range of sizes, from #14 to #3/0, and the smaller sizes are used for sea trout on the west coast of Scotland.

Variations on Ally's Shrimp include the addition of crystal hair to the tail and the use of red, yellow, green, lilac, black and brown for the tail and collar hackle. On the Pacific coast of North America, red and purple – the colours often used in other steelhead patterns – are the preferred colours, although the General Practitioner remains the prawn pattern of choice.

FISHING THE SHRIMP

The fly was intended for use at the end of the season when the temperatures are falling and the salmon generally respond to more showy flies, but it has proven to be a fly for all times of the year, regardless of changes in water level or temperature. It can also be fished at any depth, from riverbed to within a few inches of the surface, but action can be all important. When a prawn has to move fast it flicks its tail under its body and propels itself backwards in bursts through the water. Short strips and pauses that simulate a creature in escape mode can help to elicit a response from the fish.

Klinkhåmer

YEAR: 1984   **FLY TYER:** Hans van Klinken   **LOCATION:** Glomma River, Norway

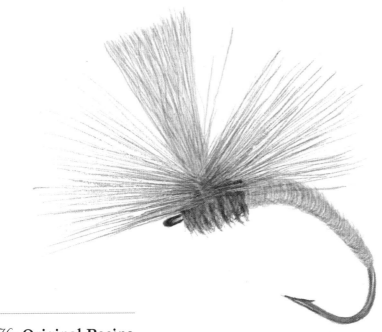

The **Original Recipe**

Hook
Wet fly/emerger, #8–#14

Thread
Light brown tying thread

Wing/Post
Tan poly yarn

Abdomen
Fine tan dubbing

Thorax
Peacock herl

Parachute
Brown cock hackle

The creation of the Klinkhåmer Special by Dutchman Hans van Klinken is an object lesson in identifying a problem, gathering information and coming up with a solution. This highly effective half-wet, half-dry emerging caddis pattern created a new class of flies and led to the development of a range of hooks specifically designed for it.

Hans took up fly fishing in 1971 at the age of 15, and was very soon undertaking solo journeys to fish the wilder parts of Norway, Sweden and Finland. He began fly tying in 1976 and focussed particularly on parachute and emerger patterns, as well as realistic nymphs. While fishing for grayling he was doing as a friend had advised him and fishing large patterns well sunk in the surface layer. He had been soaking dry flies to achieve this, and they had been working well, but Hans wanted to come up with something new. The inspiration came from a large and strongly curved caddis larva that he found in the stomach of a grayling, and in order to imitate this on the surface Hans tied a slim body of light tan dubbing right down to the bend on a large grub hook and gave his creation an upright poly yarn wing – offering excellent visibility – and a heavy duty parachute hackle.

Hans van Klinken, who lives in the Netherlands, has been tying flies since his early 20s, and has given fly tying lectures, classes and workshops across Europe, Asia and North America, as well as contributing to many books on the subject.

In his own words, 'On the 27th of June 1984, my first Klinkhåmer Special landed in the surface film of Norway's mighty Glomma River.'

The new fly floated well even in fast-moving broken water, with the majority of the hook hanging deep and almost perpendicular through the surface layer, and to Hans's astonishment the fish took the fly aggressively. He landed three grayling in short order and then set about fine tuning his new pattern.

Naming it the L.T. (Light Tan) Caddis, Hans gave the fly as slim an abdomen as possible using poly dubbing and added a peacock herl thorax. The standard hackle for the original pattern is a large blue dun. The fly changed its identity a few years later when Hans wrote an article for a Dutch fly fishing magazine and the legendary fly tyer Hans de Groot, who was on the editorial staff, renamed it in Hans's honour and gave it a Scandinavian flavour. The accent over the 'a' in Klinkhåmer has now largely been dropped.

GRAYLING AND MUCH MORE

Hans soon found that the pattern worked especially well for large grayling, which tend to push high-floating dry flies aside when they go to take them. He believes this is a result of the grayling's protruding lower lip, which is designed primarily for bottom feeding, but the fish take the 'deep surface hanging emerger' much more easily and the pattern produces a far higher proportion of hook-ups.

Hans had success with his fly throughout Europe, for both grayling and trout, and then took Atlantic salmon on larger versions in Newfoundland. The fly has since become popular around the world from Australia and New Zealand to Russia and North America.

HOOKS AND VARIATIONS

Although the large grub hook suited the pattern, Hans worked with manufacturers to develop the perfect hook with the right bend and a wide gape. Several such hooks are now available, some with a steady long curve, and others with an extreme bend part way back from the eye so that the hackle and thorax lie flat on the water while the abdomen curves dramatically downwards.

Seen from below, the Klinkhåmer presents a distinctive footprint on the water and an enticing profile.

Klinkhåmers today tend to be tied in smaller sizes than the originals, and in a huge range of colours to match a variety not only of different caddis but also upwinged emergers as well as terrestrials. Further variations on the theme include dubbing for the thorax, a turkey biot segmented abdomen, a foam wing post and a CDC soft hackle for smaller patterns. It's the shape that counts!

Sharing the Praise

Hans van Klinken graciously refuses to take all the credit for the Klinkhåmer pattern because several fly tyers came up with very similar ideas independently. Among these are the American Mike Monroe, who wrote about his 'Paratilt' in 1979, Tomas Olsen of Sweden, who developed a wingless deep hanging emerger in 1983 and another American, Roy Richardson, who produced a fly similar to the Klinkhåmer in 1986.

Holy Mackerel

YEAR: 1985   **FLY TYER:** Steve Abel   **LOCATION:** California, USA

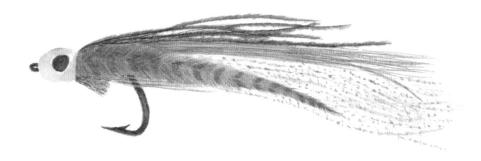

The Original Recipe

Hook
Saltwater, #8/0

Thread
Chartreuse tying thread

Body
Peacock ice chenille

Wing
White synthetic fibre

Topping
Silver holographic and blue synthetic fibre, peacock herl

Sides
Blue-dyed grizzly hackles

Beard
Red flash fibre

Head
Hot glue with doll eyes

Steve Abel's Mackerel is the largest in a family of flies that he developed in the 1980s and early 1990s for big-game saltwater fishing. The Abel flies rely on coloration, shading, big eyes and reflective artificial materials to represent vulnerable baitfish, and between them they have brought their creator a number of world records.

ABEL ANCHOVY

An experienced machinist, Steve Abel developed his own brand of high quality big-game fly reels in the 1980s and went on to design trout and steelhead reels as well as a range of other fishing accessories. He also turned his hand to fly design after noticing that when game fish such as tuna, wahoo, shark and striped bass were feeding, the water would be shimmering with clouds of glittering scales from the dead and wounded baitfish, and this would attract more feeders. In creating what was to become the Abel Anchovy he used a variety of natural materials, such as peacock herl and bucktail, but he also included various synthetics to give his fly that iridescent sparkle. The head was finished off with epoxy resin and over-sized eyes, and the resin was later replaced by less messy hot glue.

GROWING BIGGER

He soon added a tarpon-style version of the Anchovy with a long head and the majority of the materials tied in at the rear of the hook, and a wahoo version with a Mylar® tubing body. The slightly larger Abel Sardine followed and then the Abel Holy Mackerel, up to 8in (20cm) long. Both the Sardine and the Mackerel follow the same basic pattern of peacock herl, bucktail and light-catching artificial fibres, but these flies also have a long grizzly hackle on each side, lime green in the case of the Sardine and teal blue for the Mackerel to simulate the striped flanks of this glistening fish. Some tyers add a red gill flash at the throat.

Steve has taken world record blue and mako shark, wahoo (below) and skipjack tuna on his own flies. Around the world they have caught every kind of game fish from peacock bass and dorado to Pacific salmon, tarpon and sailfish.

Polish Woven Nymph

YEAR: 1986   **FLY TYER:** Anon.   **LOCATION:** Poland

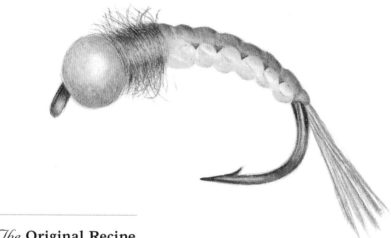

The Original Recipe

Hook
Gammarus hook in sizes #8–#16

Tail
Feather fibres

Head
Copper bead

Upper body
Brown yarn or embroidery thread

Underbody
Lead wire

Lower body
Yellow yarn or embroidery thread

Thread
Fire orange

Thorax
Synthetic peacock dub

A method of fishing fast-sinking nymphs directly beneath the rod tip was introduced to the world by the Polish fly fishing team when the championship was held in their country in 1984. The technique was adopted and, one might say, perfected by the Czech fly fishing team in subsequent years, and 'Czech nymphing' has since become an extremely popular and productive way to fish. There is now a cornucopia of flies specifically designed for this method, and the Polish Woven Nymph is a great example.

CZECH NYMPHING

The basis for the method is the fact that in many rivers the vast majority of the available food items, in the form of the immature stages of caddisflies, mayflies, stoneflies, midges etc., as well as freshwater shrimps, are to be found among the rocks, stones and mud of the riverbed, and this is where the fish are feeding. Czech nymphing is designed to reach these fish by using a slim, weighted nymph to carry a team of three flies into the feeding zone essentially without the use of the fly line. The angler keeps in direct contact with the flies by casting slightly upstream and then following the flies downstream with the rod tip, the leader being kept taut and the rod being held out over the water with the arm extended. At the end of the drift the flies are lifted away from the bottom – putting one in mind of the Leisenring Lift or Frank Sawyer's Induced Take – and the line is again cast a short distance upstream. The method was developed primarily for grayling, but it also works well for brown and rainbow trout, and European species such as chub, roach and barbel are fished for in this way, too.

Many of the flies used in Czech nymphing are designed to simulate the colour, shape and lustre of freshwater shrimps, or scuds. They are weighted to get down to the feeding zone in fast-flowing rivers.

It is an ideal way to fish through fast-moving and pocket water, and much of the skill lies in being able to detect a take, which may only be indicated by the slightest hesitation of the line. A short coloured section is often built into the leader to aid in detection. Generally very little, if any, fly line extends beyond the tip of the rod, but the method can be used at greater distances with a floating line, watching the tip of the fly line for signs of a strike.

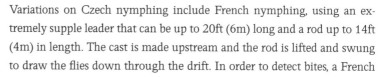

The line used in European nymphing often incorporates fluorescent monofilament as an indicator.

Variations on Czech nymphing include French nymphing, using an extremely supple leader that can be up to 20ft (6m) long and a rod up to 14ft (4m) in length. The cast is made upstream and the rod is lifted and swung to draw the flies down through the drift. In order to detect bites, a French Indicator, a spirally wound section of hi-vis monofilament, is tied between the leader and the tippet to act as an indicator. When a fish takes the nymph, the indicator stretches, alerting the angler but without spooking the fish.

Spanish nymphing takes the concept even further, with leaders up to 30ft (9m) in length. In both French and Spanish nymphing the line is fished less taut than in Czech nymphing.

THE POLISH FLY

The unique feature of the Polish Woven Nymph is, as its name suggests, the shuttle weaving of the contrasting back and underbody threads. The darker yarn goes back and forth across the top of the fly while the lighter one zigzags underneath, the two crossing each time they meet at the side. The effect is a caddis larva-like fly with a highly segmented body (that can be augmented further by ribbing) that also gives the impression of gills or legs along the sides. The slim body, bead head and lead-wrapped hook shank enable the woven nymph to sink down through the water column extremely fast, but in slower water a lighter fly is preferred as it behaves more naturally in the drift. Woven nymphs are tied in colours and sizes appropriate to the naturals, and there are versions in which coloured wire is used instead of yarn. The same construction method can also be used for other larvae such as stoneflies.

CZECH NYMPHS

The broader category of Czech nymphs, sometimes known by the Czech name of Bobesh, have much in common with the Polish Woven Nymph, being slim and heavy and tied on curved, gammarus-style hooks, but they generally have bodies of natural or synthetic dubbing and a shell back of stretchy and reflective material, as well as a ribbing of monofilament or wire. Czech nymphs originally represented natural mayflies, caddis and, commonly, freshwater shrimps, or scuds, but over the years there has been a trend towards introducing coloured hot spots and also more vivid colour combinations.

Traditional nymphs, such as the Hare's Ear and the Pheasant Tail, are also used in Czech nymphing.

SO WHAT'S NEW?

No doubt a good many Americans are reading this and thinking, 'This Czech nymphing is just short-line high-sticking! What about Ted Fay?' Good point. His story starts around the time when G.E.M. Skues was trying to persuade English anglers to fish nymphs in the upper layers of the chalk streams.

In the 1920s, a Native American fishing guide called Theodore Laverne 'Ted' Towendolly of Dunsmuir, California, was using weighted nymph patterns. His Burlap Nymph and Black Bomber, with hook shanks wrapped in lead wire, were designed to get down to the riverbed through the fast water of the Upper Sacramento River, in California, to where the trout were feeding. Towendolly introduced these nymphs and a method of fishing them to another Dunsmuir angler, Ted Fay, who developed the technique that has become known as short-line high-stick nymphing. He also created further weighted nymphs in various colours to mimic the naturals. Many anglers learned this devastatingly effective method through his guiding services and through discussions at Ted Fay's Fly Shop (which still exists), and high-sticking remains a popular way of fishing accessible pocket water in the USA.

In 1973, Larry Green, the then West Coast field editor of *Field & Stream*, wrote an article about Ted Fay in which he said, 'Working only a small section of stream directly in front of where he's wading, Ted slaps the two weighted nymphs of different patterns into the head of the riffle and follows through with the tip of his 8ft (2.4m) rod directly above his two drifting nymphs. He would rather work in swift water up to his armpits than make a long cast.' Ted Fay also tied a big and obvious knot where his fly line attached to the leader, to act as an indicator. This was more than a decade before Czech nymphing became popular, but it sounds awfully familiar.

Clouser Minnow

YEAR: 1988   **FLY TYER:** Bob Clouser   **LOCATION:** Pennsylvania, USA

The Original Recipe

Hook
Saltwater, #4–1/0

Tail
White or dyed bucktail

Thread
Strong tying thread

Wing
Darker dyed bucktail

Eyes
Dumbbell eyes sized to suit

Head
Varnished tying thread

In the mid 1990s, Lefty Kreh described this fly as 'the most important and effective underwater fly developed in the past 20 years'. His own Deceiver, of course, was created more than 20 years earlier but, like that fly, Bob Clouser's Minnow has become a multi-purpose pattern, capable of being tuned – through colour, size, weight and materials – to fit the bill in a whole spectrum of fishing situations.

FROM FRESH TO SALT

Whereas the Deceiver started life in the ocean and travelled upstream, the Clouser Deep Minnow, as Lefty Kreh dubbed it, grew out of Bob Clouser's experiments with bucktail streamers for smallmouth bass in the Susquehanna River in Pennsylvania and has since found its way into the box of virtually every sea-going fly angler.

THE EYES HAVE IT

In the mid 1980s, Bob Clouser – a fishing guide, fly tyer and tackle shop owner in Middletown, PA – had already tried attaching split shot to the hook shanks of streamers to get them down into the zone, so when he received packets of the new dumbbell eyes from the Wapsi Fly Company he put them to use.

The tying of the heavy dumbbell eyes, originally in plain metal but nowadays available in a range of colours, are the key to the success of the Clouser Minnow.

It took three years of trial and error to come up with the winning formula, based on an essentially simple bucktail streamer, and the key was in the positioning of the eyes. In the Clouser Minnow, the heavy dumbbell eyes are set almost one third of the way back from the hook eye, and they are mounted on what we normally think of as the top of the hook. The effects of this position are twofold. Firstly, the weight of the eyes causes the fly to swim hook point up, reducing the chances of hooking weed when working the fly close to the bottom. Secondly, the fly is balanced in such a way that a stripping retrieve imparts a realistic up and down darting motion to the fly without causing it to dive and rise in an unnatural way, which is what happens when the eyes are at the front.

As Lefty Kreh once said, 'If I had to choose only one fly to fish, for any species, anywhere in the world, it would be the Clouser Minnow.' In 1994 he wrote that he had caught 63 species of fish on a Clouser. That figure has now risen to at least 87.

Upside-Down Fly

YEAR: 1989   **FLY TYER:** Oliver Edwards   **LOCATION:** Yorkshire, England

𝒯𝒽𝑒 **Original Recipe**

Hook
K3A Swedish dry fly, #10–#14

Thread
Brown tying thread

Tail
Pheasant tail fibres

Wings
Dyed mallard flank

Body
Fine dry fly dubbing

Hackle
Dyed grizzly hackle

When it comes to dry flies that represent mayfly duns, there is always one glaring problem. No matter how realistically the fly presents the triggers to which the fish respond – the points of the hackle indenting the water surface and refracting the light, the outline of the wings above the body – there is always that unsightly hook penetrating the water and hanging unnaturally beneath the fly. The Upside-Down Fly offers a solution, and Oliver Edwards' Mayfly is a particularly elegant example.

PROBLEM SOLVING

The idea of having the point of the hook uppermost is not a new one. Robert Venables, writing in the mid 1600s (*The Experienced Angler*), in his instructions for tying an artificial fly, says, '…then I clip away those [feathers] that are upon the back of the hook, that so, if it be possible, the point of the hook may be forced by the feathers left on the inside of the hook, to swim upwards…'. He placed the wings of the fly on the inside of the hook, but he was not talking about a dry fly.

There were several attempts at upside-down dry flies in the late 19th and early 20th centuries, but it wasn't until the 1970s that a truly workable pattern was developed. Two British fly tyers, anglers and authors, John Goddard and Brian Clarke, took the Parachute Dun, or Paradun, as their starting point and set out to solve not the problems mentioned above but a different one. Parachute patterns, such as the Parachute Adams (see page 104), have the hackle wound horizontally around the upright wing post and this creates an excellent 'footprint' on the surface of the water, but the hackle is necessarily above the body of the fly whereas the legs of the natural are below

A Scientific Approach

John Goddard died in December 2012. In an obituary, his friend and co-author of *The Trout and the Fly*, Brian Clarke, wrote, 'It is probably true to say that, more than any other British writer in the 20th century, John Goddard persuaded anglers at large that a knowledge of entomology could be a huge advantage when trying to catch trout on artificial flies. He not only designed a veritable hatch of imitative patterns based on his own observations, but adapted the dressings of others and wrote extensively on methods for fishing them.'

it. Goddard and Clarke wanted to create the footprint while keeping the body clear of the water, as is the case in many naturals, in order to fool more difficult 'educated' trout. Their solution involved having the hook point above the water's surface.

UPSIDE-DOWN (USD) PARADUN

In its original form, the fly that they created had a tail of three muskrat whiskers well splayed out, a body of heron herl and wings of body feather tips tied on the inside of the hook, but the key lies in the way the parachute hackle is tied in on the 'back' of the hook. Before the body and wings are tied in, a loop of 4lb (1.8kg) monofilament is whipped to the top of the shank with the long free end extending over the eye. The wings are then tied in, angled slightly forwards. Using a gallows tool, the loop is then pulled upwards to create the post and the hackle is wound around its base. The loop is then released, the tip of the hackle is pulled through the loop and the loop is pulled tight to secure it before completing the body. The aerodynamics of the fly are such that it will generally land the correct way up, with the parachute hackle on the water surface and the wings in the air.

The USD is a highly effective fly, but it didn't really catch on, largely because, as Goddard and Clarke freely admitted, it is difficult to tie and because the highly selective trout for which it was designed are relatively rare or, some contend, don't exist at all.

PATTERSON'S FUNNEL DUN

A much simpler version of the USD dun was created a few years later by another British fly tyer, Neil Patterson. The key element in this style of fly (which can be tied in a range of colours and sizes, with or without a duck-flank wing) is the forward-facing, stiff and oversized hackle that forms, as

'John Goddard, the English writer, whom I regard as one of the best trout fishermen I have ever accompanied, gave me some of these to try. Under very difficult conditions, I believe that an upside-down fly will out fish either a conventional or parachute dry fly....Standard dries often have the hook protruding below the surface and are easily visible to the trout. Upside-down flies have the hook well above the surface and pretty much hidden by the fly body.'
Lefty Kreh, *Lefty Kreh's Ultimate Guide to Fly Fishing* (2003)

the name suggests, a funnel over the eye of the hook. The hackle fibre tail is tied in partway round the bend of the hook and, together with the shape of the hackle, this helps the fly to land point up in the same way as the USD Paradun. The long hackle places a large 'footprint' on the water and the angled tail helps the fly to sit on the surface in the right position.

THE HOOK FOR THE JOB

The introduction of the Partridge K3A hook in 1979 marked a major step forward in upside-down flies. Designed by leading fly tyers Nils E. Eriksson and Gunnar Johnson, the 'Swedish dry fly hook' has a kink in the shank where the parachute hackle is tied, and it naturally rides point up. Eriksson and Johnson designed several patterns based on this hook, as did the American fly tyer, fanatical angler and prolific writer Gary LaFontaine, but whereas the focus of upside-down efforts had so far been on mayfly patterns, he channelled his energies into the sedge or caddis.

The Partridge K3A hook was specifically designed with a kink so that a hackle tied around the shank would be parallel to the water surface.

Like Clarke and Goddard, LaFontaine was a keen entomologist with a firm belief in the need to match the hatch, and he produced a series of some fifteen upside-down 'Dancing Caddis' patterns, with dubbed fur bodies, backward-swept deer hair wings and hackles of rooster hackle, in a whole range of colour combinations. He later created the Simplified Dancing Caddis, adapting these patterns to be tied on a standard hook.

Rooster hackles are typically used for dry flies because they are stiff, non-absorbent and support the fly on the water.

HEAD OVER HEELS

All these attempts at designing a hook-point-up fly placed the head and tail of the fly in the traditional positions – at the eye and the bend of the hook respectively. In the mid 1970s, when he was in his early twenties, Irish fly tyer Roy Christie rethought the whole idea and turned things around. His Avon Special Emerger has the tail whisk pointing over the eye of the hook, the hackle wound horizontally around the hook bend and the wing pointing upwards from the bend at right angles to the point of the hook. The fly floats with the body submerged, suspended in the surface film by the parachute hackle, and the wing makes the fly highly visible to the angler.

In the mid 1990s, professional fly tyer Giuliano Masetti applied similar back-to-front thinking to a dry fly style – the Waterwisp® – and also designed the hook to suit his pattern. The Waterwisp® hook has a large gape to help solve the hook-up issue and the eye is in the same plane as the bend of the hook so that the hook can be fixed in the vice by the eye and tied in reverse.

'A sad fact of modern fly-fishing is that so much of the lore is geared to one insect, mayflies, that the typical angler has difficulty adapting his methods to the feeding that occurs during a caddisfly hatch. He is conditioned to fish his flies to simulate the typical habits of a mayfly, not a caddisfly.' **Gary LaFontaine,** **Caddisflies (1989)**

EDWARDS SWEDISH MAYFLY

The British fly tyer Oliver Edwards also experimented with the K3A Swedish dry fly hook in the late 1980s and his original mayfly pattern appeared in John Roberts' *A Guide to River Trout Flies* in 1989. Many variations on his *Ephemera danica* (green drake) pattern have been tied since but, as Edwards himself says, the upside-down fly has probably had its day. The reasons for this are partly to do with the low hook-up rate for the upturned fly, not only because the hook point is on top but also because the wing can tend to occlude it. Edwards found that this can be partly overcome by twisting the hook to offset the point, but the kink in the shank also makes the hook rather springy, and these particular hooks are no longer easily obtainable.

Aside from such dry patterns as his Footprint Dun, a low-riding smooth-water pattern with six distinct spindly legs, Oliver Edwards is probably best known for his amazingly lifelike nymphs, larvae and shrimp patterns, and especially his Rhyacophila Larva, or Green Rockworm, one of the largest of the caddis family and an excellent pattern for Czech nymphing. As well as being the author of *Oliver Edwards' Flytyer's Masterclass*, Edwards is also the creator of the *Essential Skills* and *Essential Patterns* series of instructional fly fishing and fly tying DVDs.

Oliver Edwards holds a wild brown trout caught in a lake section of the Big Laxa River in Iceland on one of his own flies. He describes his visit to this remote location as the most exciting wild brown trout fishing he has ever encountered.

Syl's Midge

YEAR: 1991   **FLY TYER:** Sylvester Nemes   **LOCATION:** Montana, USA

The Original Recipe

Hook
Nymph, #12–#20

Thread
Black tying thread

Body
Three strands of
peacock herl

Hackle
Hungarian partridge or
Brahma hen

Head:
Varnished black
tying thread

In the decades after the publication of Leisenring and Hidy's work on flymphs, the trend in North American fly tying and fly fishing was very largely towards dry flies and ever more realistic patterns. The impressionistic soft-hackled wets were relegated to a back seat by all but a dedicated minority, but among those who kept the faith was angler, fly tyer and writer Sylvester Nemes, who has done more than anyone else to keep the soft hackle alive and bring its qualities into focus in the USA. Syl's Midge is a superb example of the simplicity and efficacy of this style of fly.

INFLUENTIAL WRITING

Nemes' first book, *The Soft-Hackled Fly,* was published in 1975, and in it he traced the whole history of this genre, especially the North Country flies that Pritt had written about, as well as showing how modern materials and tying methods could be applied to them. The wealth of information and his easy writing style won him and the soft-hackled fly many followers, and signalled the start of a swing away from the quest for entomological exactness and towards a more relaxed approach to fly impersonation.

In 1991 he published *Soft-Hackled Fly Imitations,* and in this book, which looked at matching specific North American hatches, he gave instructions for many of his own patterns, including Syl's Midge. His other works include *The Soft-Hackled Fly Addict* (1993), *Two Centuries of Soft-Hackled Flies* (2003) and *Spinners* (2006). Also in 2006, an expanded version of his first book, now entitled *The Soft-Hackled Fly and Tiny Soft Hackles: A Trout Fisherman's Guide,* appeared, more highly illustrated and with more patterns, including ten chapters on tying midges and other tiny flies.

Sylvester Nemes was stationed in Hampshire, England, in 1944 and there he fished soft hackles on the famous River Test. Back in the USA he developed his own patterns for the Madison, Missouri and Yellowstone rivers.

'I have been called evangelistic by some anglers in my attempts to establish the soft hackle as a true, American angling form. I hope this book continues the crusade.'
Sylvester Nemes, *The Soft-Hackled Fly Addict*

In terms of both the materials and the method of tying, this fly could hardly be simpler. Looking somewhat like a bulbous spider pattern, Syl's Midge has a body of twisted peacock herl that keeps the barbs of the soft Hungarian partridge hackle pushed out and able to waft and pulse in the current as the fly floats downstream. It is designed to be fished in the surface layers 'under the hatch', in the phrase coined by Ernest Herbert 'Polly' Rosborough in his book *Tying and Fishing the Fuzzy Nymphs*, published in 1965. His theory was that even when adult insects are on the surface, fish will often more readily take nymphs and drowned or crippled adults beneath the surface, and the experience of many soft-hackled devotees supports this.

Although this fly represents the tiny midge, Nemes himself maintained that there was no need to tie it in any sizes smaller than a #16, as this had proved just as effective as a #22, which is a great deal harder to tie and less likely to produce a hook-up.

BROADER APPLICATIONS

Sylvester Nemes' has not been a lone voice over the last 40 years. Writers such as W.S. Roger Fogg, Dave Hughes and Allen McGee are among the many who have lent their support to the cause of re-examining the history of the soft hackle and developing new patterns, sometimes in combination with new materials.

Anglers and fly tyers from many different areas of the sport have been adding vitality to their creations by extending the use of soft hackles into flies designed for everything from largemouth bass to saltwater species such as bonefish. Large versions of North Country spider patterns have long been used by steelheaders in the Pacific Northwest, and Loren Williams' Steelhead Pat, which has a hackle of grey and brown Hungarian partridge, takes both Atlantic salmon and Great Lakes steelhead.

Harking Back

In his supplement to Izaak Walton's *The Compleat Angler* entitled *Being Instructions How To Angle for a Trout or Grayling in a Clear Stream*, Charles Cotton gives the ingredients for flies that are to be fished in May and says, 'There is also in this month a fly called the Peacock-Fly; the body made of a whirl of a peacock's feather, with a red head, and wings of a mallard's feather'. If a soft breast feather is intended, this would be a similar fly to Syl's Midge.

THE SOFT-HACKLED DRY

Dry flies are traditionally wound with a cock hackle, either around the hook shank or in a parachute form, and the stiff fibres help the fly to float, act to stabilise the fly and give the impression of feet on the water's surface. They also hold the fly in the surface film and help it to move with the current, reducing unnatural drag. The one things that those fibres do not do is look like the flexible, mobile legs of a living insect.

A fly called the Jingler, reputedly a 19th-century Scottish pattern, solves this by combining a dry fly cock hackle and all its useful qualities with a soft Hungarian partridge hackle. The partridge, tied in with the concave side facing forwards, is wound in front of the dry fly hackle or through it so that it helps to support the soft fibres. The partridge hackle fibres are slightly longer than those of the cock hackle and when the fly is resting on the water these 'legs' move in the current. The effect is that of a mayfly emerger or dun trapped or crippled and struggling in the surface film, and the fly certainly appears to possess a key trigger that elicits a response from the fish.

The Jingler, which has burst on to the UK scene from obscurity in the last decade, is commonly tied as a March Brown with a dubbed hare's ear body, or as a Large Dark Olive with a thread or quill body. The English angler and guide Jon Barnes, who is a strong advocate of spider patterns, ties a version of the Jingler that has a CDC wing. His Soft Hackle Dry Fly represents small to medium mayflies and caddisflies.

The Jingler, seen here in its March Brown and LDO versions tied by Rob Smith of North Country Flies, is extremely effective during a hatch and has gained many keen admirers in the last few years.

Ice Cream Cone

YEAR: 1992   **FLY TYER:** Kelly Davidson   **LOCATION:** British Columbia, Canada

The Original Recipe

Hook
Scud or curved shank nymph,
#8–#20

Head
White metal, glass or
plastic bead

Thread
Black tying thread

Body
Black plastic or Krystal Flash
over tapered thread underbody

Rib
Thin red wire

Coating
Hard-setting gloss varnish

The fishing of chironomid pupa patterns in still waters for trout has a relatively short history, and initially the methods of tying artificials were broadly similar to those for other flies, using dubbing and other soft materials. It was in 1992 that Kelly Davison, a fishing guide and outfitter in Coquitlam, near Vancouver, decided to try a new approach and created an entirely new family of flies using a distinctive white bead head and a ribbed thread body.

BRITISH STILL WATERS

Trout may well have been perceiving small spider and nymph patterns as chironomids for decades, but the first true pupa pattern was reputedly tied in the 1920s by Dr H.A. Bell for fishing Blagdon Lake, one of Britain's first reservoirs. After studying the life cycle of the chironomid there he designed the Blagdon Buzzer with a black wool body, gold tinsel ribbing to provide the segmentation, and a tuft of white wool at the head to represent the gills. The pattern is still in use today.

Still waters in England were traditionally the 'coarse' angler's territory, but the introduction of trout to reservoirs and lakes has attracted the fly fishers and led to the development of new flies.

By the 1960s and 1970s the number of reservoirs and managed still-water trout fisheries in Britain had increased considerably and so had interest in this form of fishing. Arthur Cove had already introduced his pupa-like version of the Pheasant Tail Nymph, and Frank Sawyer himself had brought out the Bowtie Buzzer, which hangs vertically in the surface film. Being held on only by the gill-like bowtie at the end of the line rather than a knot, it swings loosely on a gentle retrieve and resembles a midge pupa breaking through the surface tension.

Writers such as C.F. Walker, Brian Clarke and John Goddard introduced the angling public to the world of chironomid fishing and to new patterns, including Goddard's Suspender

The Life Cycle of the Chironomid

Given that a significant proportion of a stillwater trout's diet can be composed of chironomids – as much as 40 per cent in the course of a year – it is surprising how long it took the fishing community to switch on to this enormous family of insects, with an estimated 10,000 species world wide. Known as buzzers in the UK, chironomids are mosquito-like non-biting midges that spend the majority of their lives in water – as eggs, larvae and pupae – before emerging as winged adults.

The eggs of the chironomid – up to 3,000 per adult female – are laid on the surface of the water and then sink to the bottom. In some species, the larvae that hatch from the eggs create tubular homes in the sediment, where there can be up to 4,000 larvae per square foot of lake bed. These larvae, which stay close to the lake bed, tend to have some red coloration due to the presence of haemoglobin, and these are referred to as bloodworms. Bloodworm patterns can be as simple as a red-wrapped hook fished just off the bottom. In other species the larvae are free swimming and range in colour from very pale through green to brown.

The pupae, which are much larger than those of mosquitoes, are of much greater interest to anglers. When conditions are right and water temperatures are sufficiently high the larvae pupate and thousands of them ascend slowly through the water column. Trout and other fish, as well as aquatic insects such as water boatmen and *Dytiscus* larvae, feed on them voraciously at these times, and chironomid or buzzer fishing almost always refers to fishing patterns that mimic this stage of the insect's life.

Once at the surface the pupa lies horizontally and the adult, looking very much like a winged version of the pupa, emerges into the air from the split pupal shuck. The adults fly to the shoreline where they mate in huge clouds – emitting the familiar buzz that gives them their English name – and the females soon return to the water to lay their eggs, often forming clumps of several flies in a group. Fish feed on these egg-laying females too, and small dry patterns such as Griffith's Gnat can work well at this time.

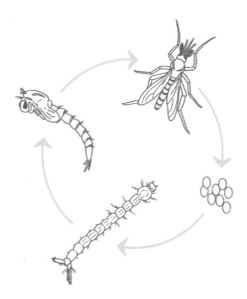

The larva and pupa of the non-biting midge, or chironomid, are a major food source for fish in still waters, and anglers make use of a wide range of artificial flies that mimic these.

Midge Pupa, which uses a foam ball to keep it almost horizontal in the surface film, like a midge about to emerge. Highly effective on still waters, it soon proved successful on rivers used in very small sizes when trout and grayling are taking tiny surface flies, or 'smutting'. At around the same time, Geoffrey Bucknall used black and white horsehair to create a striped pattern called the Footballer Buzzer.

By the end of the 1970s buzzer fishing was firmly established in Britain and it remains a mainstay of the stillwater — and particularly the reservoir — angler there today.

NORTH AMERICAN DEVELOPMENTS

This style of angling has had a strangely separate and yet parallel course of development in North America, particularly in the Pacific Northwest and most markedly in British Columbia, Canada, where new patterns abound and techniques are constantly refined. Little wonder, then, that this was the birthplace of a style of chironomid that has revolutionised this class of fly.

Aside from a few largely unsuccessful attempts, there was little in the way of North American chironomid fishing in the first half of the

Tunkwa Lake, one of BC's richest, is famous for its huge chironomid hatches in the spring. Chosen as the venue for World and National Fly Fishing Championships, it holds plenty of rainbows over 5lb (2.3 kg).

This TDC, tied by Steve Schalla of the Fly Fishing the Sierra website, has a body of black beaver dubbing in place of the black wool and retains the white ostrich herl gills. It is still a popular pattern and has served as the basis for many variations.

twentieth century. It wasn't until the early 1960s that Dick Thompson, a federal fisheries biologist in Washington State, created a breakthrough pattern in a moment of frustration. Fishing a small high desert lake south of Ephrata with a friend, he watched fish rising everywhere without any sign of a hatch and was unable to persuade the fish to take any of the usual favourites. When, at long last, he caught one he examined its stomach contents 'and found lots of black, white-striped pupae with little white collars near the head'. Sounds familiar? With his vice clamped to the steering wheel of his car he did his best to simulate them, using black wool with a silver rib and a little white ostrich herl at the head. It was an immediate hit, and the TDC (Thompson's Delectable Chironomid) was soon being used by members of the Washington Fly Fishing Club and then across the region after Thompson published an article describing the fly. Many anglers, however, gave up on it because it wasn't working for them, and it took a while before fishing techniques – essentially a painfully slow retrieve and new ways of placing the fly at the right depth – caught up with the TDC.

Other chironomid patterns soon followed, and most of them included the white fibre gills that seemed to be a vital part of the attraction for trout. These are fiddly to tie, and it was Kelly Davison, a BC fishing guide and outfitter, who in 1992 came up with the novel and much simpler idea of giving his chironomids a small white bead head (initially he got his sons to use white spray paint on a batch of black beads strung out on mono line, which proved extremely messy). When he tested his creation on one of the many lakes around Kamloops, which are famous for their chironomid hatches, he had barely begun lowering the fly into the water when it was taken by a trout.

As well as having gills, pupae also appear to accumulate a small amount of gas beneath the skin, which may assist them in their ascent and serve to free the burgeoning adult from the pupal shuck, and this can give the pupa a lustre and degree of translucency. The white bead and shiny surface of the Davison's artificial may also emulate these characteristics. Whatever the case, his Ice Cream Cones (also know as Snow Cones or Snocones) have given rise to an entire family of flies in every size and colour and they are found in almost every chironomid angler's fly box.

It is not surprising that both Dick Thompson and Kelly Davison created their chironomid patterns for use in high-altitude lakes in the rain shadow of the Cascades mountain range. There are literally hundreds of these lakes, stretching from northern California to southern British Columbia, and they offer ideal conditions for chironomids – fertile, nutrient-rich waters with silty lake beds and a long growing season –and in many lakes the abundant midge larvae and pupae provide trout with the bulk of their diet, virtually all year round.

Patterns for these highly productive lakes, some of which hold rainbows up to 10lb (4.5kg), have been developed by tyers such as Brian Chan and Phil Row- ley. As a provincial fisheries biologist, Brian managed the region's recreational stillwater trout fisheries for more than 30 years, and he has applied his extensive knowledge of trout ecology and entomology to fly tying and fly fishing techniques. Both he and Phil Rowley, a professional fly tyer and a member of the gold medal winning team at the Canadian Fly Fishing championships in 2007, are the authors of countless web and magazine articles, as well as several books (some of them together) and DVDs. They both offer fly fishing tuition and appear on national television, including co-hosting a fly fishing TV series. As well as some well-known chironomids, the flies they have created cover a range of stillwater patterns, including dry flies, nymphs and leeches.

Generally tied on a #10 2XL or 3XL hook, Brian Chan's Ruby Eyed Leech has a cone head in front of a red glass bead, with a maroon body of blended black and red sparkly synthetic seal dubbing.

Seen here with his long-time friend and fishing partner Phil Rowley, Brian Chan holds up a fine fly-caught Kamloops trout before returning it to the water.

Annihilator

YEAR: 1993   **FLY TYER:** Anon.   **LOCATION:** Pacific Northwest

The Original Recipe

Hook
Saltwater, #6–#8

Thread
Pink tying thread

Underbody
Fluorescent pink vinyl

Shellback / Feelers
Peacock Krystal Flash

Eye
Prismatic eye, black
on red

Coating
Two-part epoxy or
UV-setting resin

The introduction of epoxy resin into the toolkit of the fly tyer and the discovery of its possibilities have led to the development of a whole array of flies, largely – but not exclusively – for use in saltwater. When used over an underbody of natural or synthetic hair and sparkling materials such as tinsel and Flashabou, clear resin can create a very realistic sheen or a completely translucent body. The use of flowing deer hair, marabou or fine synthetic stranded material for tails, fins, legs and feelers helps to add lifelike action to hard-bodied flies such as the simple but effective Annihilator shrimp pattern.

SURF CANDY

In the 1970s many fly tyers started experimenting with epoxy resin, but one of the most creative and successful was Bob Popovics of New Jersey, USA. He initially became involved with resin in the hope of protecting a bucktail streamer so that it wouldn't be torn to shreds by the bluefish along the East Coast, and it took him several years to find a way of manipulating the wet epoxy into the bucktail fibres to achieve the desired effect. The advent of durable and light-reflecting synthetic fibres allowed him to make even better use of the properties of epoxy, and his Surf Candy – with its tough head, lifelike shimmer and flowing sinuous body – was an instant hit.

In the larger sizes, the epoxy-headed Surf Candies feature the Fleye Foil bait fish faces that Bob Popovics (below) designed to create instant realism. The bottom two flies are his Schoolies, double Surf Candies tied on keel hooks.

POP FLEYES

Over the last 30 years Popovics has been a leading light in the world of epoxy saltwater flies, coming up with a host of imaginative baitfish and eel patterns that he calls Pop Fleyes. The spelling emphasises the importance he places on eyes as a key attractor for the fish, and in the course of his experiments with various kinds of eyes he invented Fleye Foils, pre-shaped iridescent images of the sides of a baitfish head that are added to the head of the fly and then epoxied over.

Lefty Kreh has called Bob Popovics the most innovative fly tyer he has ever met, and in 1988 Popovics was inducted into the Freshwater Fishing Hall of Fame in recognition of his contribution to the sport. His Schoolie

fly – two, three or four individual Surf Candy-type flies tied on a single keel hook to represent a mini bait ball – is a great example of the lateral thinking that sets him apart.

Popovics hasn't restricted himself to flies that represent fish. His Ultra Shrimp, developed in the early 1990s, was another ground breaker with its realistic transparent body, and he has designed several squid patterns for which he has now developed stick-on Squid Foils to provide the distinctive markings of the real thing.

Nor has he restricted himself to epoxy or the range of quick-setting and UV-curing hard finish materials now available. One of the pioneers of silicone fly bodies – which may not be as indestructible as resin but are lighter, softer and easier to work with – he also designed the Siliclone Mullet in the 1990s. This baitfish fly can be made to swim at the surface as it has almost neutral buoyancy, a product of the materials – bucktail, sheep fleece and silicone – and the air that is trapped in the fleece fibres by the addition of the silicone outer layer.

THE ANNIHILATOR

Since the 1980s the Pacific Northwest has seen the development of its own range of resin flies – small shrimp, squid and baitfish patterns specifically designed for fly fishing in the surf for pink salmon, sea-run cutthroat trout and especially coho salmon, which can reach 20lb (9kg). The Annihilator, which has been around since the early 1990s and is

Fly fishing from the beach in late summer and early autumn, as the pink and coho salmon prepare to make their way upriver to spawn, is a growing sport along the northern Pacific coast.

Made entirely from synthetic materials such as vinyl, Mylar, Flashabou and epoxy resin, these small squid patterns are durable, light to cast – and effective.

popular on Vancouver Island, is generally tied on a #8 stainless steel hook with a silver tinsel underbody, a body of fluorescent pink or green vinyl, a peacock flash tail and shellback, a prismatic eye and a coat of epoxy resin. The small squid patterns, with a green or orange underbody beneath Mylar tubing, are tied on a slightly larger hook.

FRESHWATER TOO

The use of epoxy resin has never really caught on for freshwater flies, perhaps because their size makes them more difficult to work on, but there has always been a role for a clear, hard finish. Various kinds of varnish and cement have been used not only to protect whip finishes but also to create a hard carapace or shell-back, or a complete reflective outer surface in the case of chironomids. These varnishes and cements are now largely being supplanted by UV-curing one-part resins that come in various degrees of viscosity, can be applied in small quantities and can be made to set to a dry, durable and glossy finish in a matter of seconds by exposing them to UV light. They can be used to create much thicker layers than varnish will achieve, and freshwater fly tyers are constantly finding new ways to use them. In the case of chironomids, light-activated resin can be used to create transparent three-dimensional bodies with real internal detail, especially when combined with clear or coloured stretch tubing (see page 211).

Combining traditional and synthetic materials with UV-setting resin, Holger Lachmann has created these amazingly realistic scud and mayfly nymph patterns.

Tarpon Toad

YEAR: 1994   **FLY TYER:** Gary Merriman   **LOCATION:** Georgia, USA

The Original Recipe

Hook
Saltwater, #2/0

Body
Marabou

Thread
Waxed chartreuse
tying thread

Head
Enrico Puglisi fibres tied in
four sections

Tail
Rabbit strip or marabou

Eyes
Mono eyes

Gary Merriman, a fly shop owner in Atlanta, Georgia, has been hooked on bonefish and tarpon fishing in the Florida Keys since the 1970s, and in the early 1990s he began work on the fly pattern for which he is best known. The flat-headed, level-swimming Tarpon Toad, often tied in green, chartreuse and yellow, was a game changer in the world of tarpon fishing.

FLAT FORERUNNERS

When fly tyer Del Brown created the Merkin crab for permit back in the 1980s, he created a flat body of fibres that spread horizontally from the hook shank to mimic the body of the crab, and it remains a popular pattern. A few years later, Harry Spears used a similar tying method – clumps of yarn running horizontally across the hook shank but with their ends pinched flat and coated in varnish – to simulate the flat body of the toad-fish on which bonefish feed in the Florida Keys. The Tasty Toad was fished with a 12in (30cm) to 18in (45cm) strip so that the fly, with its heavy dumbbell eyes, would rise in the water and then sink back down to the bottom, but the flat body gave it a degree of glide.

WHEN HARRY MET GARY

It was this quality that Gary Merriman picked up on when he and Harry were fishing together. His innovation was to adapt the flat body form and create a neutrally buoyant fly, using black monofilament eyes, providing a marabou collar and giving his Tarpon Toad a fuller tail of rabbit fur tied skin-side up for a softer landing and more movement in the water, although marabou is now often used instead. The head – the key element – is made of several slim bunches of Enrico Puglisi (EP) fibres tied closely together across the head with figure-of-eight wraps and then trimmed to shape. The result is a hugely effective tarpon fly that truly swims in the water.

In 1984, Gary Merriman caught the largest Pacific blue marlin ever landed by a single angler – a 16ft 4in (5m) fish weighing 1,649lb (748kg). It was not recognised as a record by the International Game Fish Association because the combined length of his double-line and leader fractionally exceeded the limit set by the IGFA.

Copper John Nymph

YEAR: 1996   **FLY TYER:** John Barr   **LOCATION:** Colorado, USA

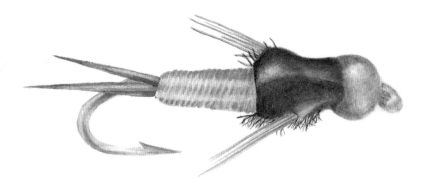

The Original Recipe

Hook
2XL, 2X heavy #10–#18

Head
Gold tungsten bead

Thread
Black tying thread

Tail
Brown goose biots

Body
Copper wire over lead wire
and thread base

Thorax
Peacock herl

Legs
Hen hackle fibres

Wing case
Epoxy over Flashabou
over Thin Skin

If you thought the Pheasant Tail Nymph was a fast sinking pattern, wait until you've tried this one. Designed by John Barr of Boulder, Colorado, the Copper John is 90 per cent metal, and no fly gets down into the zone more quickly. It represents a wide range of larvae, pupae and nymphs, from midges and sedges through mayflies and stoneflies, and in the USA it has proven as popular as the Prince Nymph or the bead-head Hare's Ear.

GOING DOWN

John tied the prototype for this fly in 1993 to use as the weight factor in a two- or three-fly rig, and over the following three years he fine-tuned it to create the version that we know today. The hook most commonly used is a heavy wire 2X long, and the shank is wrapped in lead wire behind a tungsten bead head. The body is copper wire wrapped over a smooth, tapering thread base, and the wing case is Thin Skin over a thorax of peacock herl and a strip of Flashabou, finished with epoxy to give it a little shine.

John Barr started tying flies when he was just six years old and now has a whole list of new patterns to his name, from nymphs and emergers through dries and bass surface patterns, many of which are marketed commercially.

The result is a glinting, fast-sinking, all-purpose nymph, and the colour of the copper wire can be varied to suit the hatch and the conditions. The original was natural copper, but black, chartreuse, red, silver, blue and even hot pink are very effective.

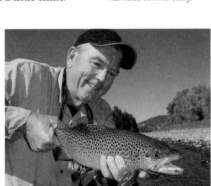

HOPPER, COPPER, DROPPER

Although the Copper John fishes well in its own right, it is most effective as part of a multi-fly rig (where more than one fly is allowed), and John recommends using his H-C-D system. This consists of a BC Hopper – a very high-floating deer hair and foam hopper pattern developed by John Barr and Charlie Craven – as both an attractor and an indicator, attached to a suitably sized Copper John by about 4ft (1.2m) of tippet and then an appropriate dropper, chosen to match the hatch, about 18in (45cm) beneath that. This enables the angler to fish to several depths, and bites can be expected on any of the three.

THE STATE OF THE ART IN 2000

*T*he first half of the 20th century saw a gradual improvement in the design of rods, reels and line, but in essence they changed little from those of the 1890s. The second half, however, was a different story. A range of new materials opened new possibilities that tackle manufacturers were quick to explore and exploit – fortunately for fly fishers.

Rods

In 1919 Dr George Parker Holden wrote in *The Idyll of the Split-Bamboo*, 'The acme of perfection in angling rods – "the rod fine-tempered with elastic spring" – is realized only in one built properly of six strips of split bamboo. In the maximum combination of the qualities of resiliency, balance, and lightness with power, quickness, and smoothness or sweetness of action, such a one is unsurpassed; and the split-bamboo rod of the best American manufacture has no superior the world over.'

The rest of the world soon caught up on rod-building techniques, and cork handles, standardised reel seats and slim 'suction joint' ferrules on multi-piece rods became the norm, but for the first half of the 20th century split cane was undoubtedly the material of choice, not only for fly rods – trout, bass and salmon – but for most kinds of freshwater and sea fishing.

The 1950s, however, were a turning point, as new materials began to take over. Fibreglass was initially developed for use in aircraft during World War II, and it soon found roles in a wide range of applications, including fishing rods, which hit the market in the 1950s. At first they were built around a wooden core, but hollow rods soon followed. Although they were no

Fishing rods and accessories that would not have looked out of place 100 years ago are still being made for anglers who take pleasure in craftsmanship.

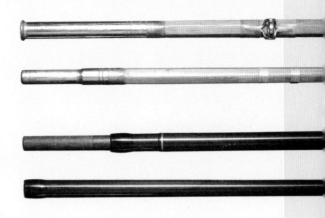

Split-cane rods more than 50 years old are still in use today, and new ones are still being made, but the majority of anglers prefer the faster action – and generally lower cost – of a graphite rod.

lighter than bamboo, the fibreglass newcomers were a great deal cheaper and far less breakable, and in the course of the 1960s and 1970s – as the technology improved – they vied with split-cane rods for supremacy.

In the 1960s, the search for strong light-weight material for military and space-race use led to the development of boron and graphite fibre materials, and by the 1970s these were being used in rod construction. Graphite soon won out over boron mainly because of cost considerations. Lighter and more powerful than fibreglass, capable of producing longer and more accurate casts, and able to reproduce some of the most desirable qualities of split cane, graphite quickly came to dominate the market.

That remains the case today, but the older materials have certainly not disappeared. In fact there has been a resurgence in the use of both bamboo and fibreglass in recent years, and with good reason.

Split cane has always had its devotees, and not just for reasons of tradition – although a good hand-built split-cane rod is undoubtedly a thing of beauty. The slower action offers delicate presentation, and a short bamboo rod has its advantages on small streams and in confined spaces where the faster action of a graphite rod can be a hindrance. Several of the top rod manu-facturers and a host of small-scale craftsmen still make split-cane rods to meet a growing demand. High quality fibreglass rods that have a similar slower action are also making a comeback.

Reels

If anything, fly reels have become simpler in the last 100 years. Gone are the geared and automatic reels, and the focus has been on making the single action reel lighter, stronger, smoother, faster on the retrieve and with great-er line capacity. To these ends, manufacturers have turned increasingly to aluminium, alloys and plastic, improved bearings and wider, large arbour spools. While the traditional click pawl system is still used on freshwater reels to

Many anglers prefer the simple but effective click pawl system (in which a spring-loaded tooth runs against a cog) to an adjustable drag mechanism.

A modern saltwater reel is made of corrosion-resistant materials and has a smooth and easily adjustable drag system for playing powerful fish.

Wood pioneered 'greased line' fishing with a fly on or close to the surface. He was extremely successful, and because the floating line required less effort to lift from the water he was able to use a shorter, 12ft (3.7m) rod that he cast single-handed. The greased line method led to a general shortening of salmon rods, and within twenty years double-handed salmon rods had given way to rods as short as 9ft or 10ft (2.75–3m) in North America.

As in the case of rods, it was the arrival of new materials that transformed fly lines in the 1950s. Nylon monofilament took a while to dethrone gut for casts and leaders (early versions were stretchy and somewhat unreliable, and gut remained in use into the 1960s), but the advent of plastic fly line brought about immediate change. Here at last was a line that could not become waterlogged, that could accurately be made in a range of tapers, weights, sink rates and colours, and that was cheaper than its predecessor. Silk line was dead in the water – almost.

prevent line overrun and to offer the fish a degree of resistance, many reels now feature some form of disc drag. Interchangeable spools are another common feature of the modern reel.

Saltwater fly reels have probably seen the greatest evolution since the 1900s, with the use of corrosion-resistant anodised aluminium, sealed bearings and, most importantly, highly efficient waterproof drag systems to control the ever stronger and larger species of fish that are being targeted by the fly angler, from bonefish and tarpon to shark and blue marlin.

Line

In many respects fly line technology has been at the heart of the developments that have taken place in rod and reel design in the course of the 1900s. At the start of the century, dressed silk lines had largely replaced horsehair, being smoother, easier to cast and more consistently tapered, but they were still prone to becoming waterlogged and would not float for long. Dry fly anglers liberally coated their lines with lanolin, while salmon anglers fished the sunk fly, but in the 1920s the English engineer A.H.E.

The modern fly line is a highly refined piece of technology, with an extremely precise weight and taper designed for specific conditions and a coating that helps it to slide through the rod rings and, in a floating line, gives added buoyancy.

Return of the Spey Rod

Spey casting, using long double-handed rods, is undergoing something of a revival in North America, largely as a result of steelhead anglers applying these techniques on the fast, wide rivers of the Pacific Northwest. Spey casting has also found renewed popularity in Europe and especially Scandinavia. Whereas the 19th-century Spey rod could be a weighty beast up to 20ft (6m) long, the modern lightweight graphite equivalent is between 11ft and 16ft (about 3 and 5m) in length, and the heavy silk lines of yesteryear have been replaced with hi-tech lines such as the Scandi(navian) Shooting Head and the Skagit Head, designed for specific conditions and fishing techniques.

The modern Spey rod comes into its own on wide rivers and where there is limited space for a backcast. Spey casting is finding renewed popularity among salmon and steelhead anglers alike.

Lingering Silk

Silk line, too, is making a comeback, in keeping with the return of the split-cane rod to which it is so well suited. Proponents of the traditional line (which several small manufacturers now produce) cite several advantages. These include the fact that silk line has no memory (unlike plastic, which can tend to coil in cold weather), and it is more dense and therefore has a smaller diameter for a given weight, so it cuts through the wind more easily and produces less disturbance on the surface of the water when it lands and when it lifts off. They admit that it requires more care and maintenance, but nothing too onerous.

Hooks

The key words in the progress of the fish hook in the 20th century are quality and variety. Metals, manufacturing techniques, sharpening methods and finishes have all improved greatly in the last 100 years to create a consistently strong, sharp and durable product.

Although there is still no single hook sizing scale, the sizing of fly tying hooks is now fairly standard, as is the system for describing the weight of the wire used and the length of the shank. Hook shapes are more diverse than they have ever been, with hooks being produced for the tying of specific patterns in some cases, and whether you are looking to tie a nymph, baitfish, caddis pupa, streamer, shrimp, bass popper, emerger or dry fly, you'll be able to find the right hook for the task.

It's gratifying to know that in 2006 *Forbes* magazine named the fish hook as one of the 20 most important tools in human history.

Deer Hair Emerger

YEAR: 2004   **FLY TYER:** Bob Wyatt   **LOCATION:** Alberta, Canada

The Original Recipe

Hook
Fine wire scud hook #10–#16

Wing
Deer hair, natural

Thread
Brown tying thread

Thorax
Hare's ear dubbing, natural

Abdomen
Hare's ear dubbing (dyed to suit)

Most artificial flies have identifiable ancestors, and many are designed to meet a particular need or serve a specific purpose, but the forebears are rarely so clearly acknowledged and the aims are seldom so clearly expressed as they are in the case of Bob Wyatt's Deer Hair Emerger. Carefully thought out and relatively simple to tie, the DHE brought the no-hackle fly to a new level – half submerged.

Born in Alberta, and an experienced fisher of the freestone rivers of western Canada and New Zealand, Bob Wyatt approached fly design from the perspective of behavioural ecology – looking at the feeding behaviour of fish as a set of evolved adaptive responses. In his controversial and highly acclaimed book *Trout Hunting: The Pursuit of Happiness*, published in 2004, he called into question the intelligence of fish and the extent to which they learn from their experiences and become 'educated'. He also examined the concept of selective feeding, which was a corner-stone of Swisher and Richards' approach in *Selective Trout*, the book that introduced their no-hackle dressings to the angling world.

To Swisher and Richards the essential triggers that spur fish to take a fly are to be found in the detail, and artificials should be as much like the natural as possible. In Wyatt's view, when fish are 'keyed in' to a particular food item, for example during a hatch, they are not checking each fly to see whether it has the right number of tail whisks but are instead responding to the broader key triggers of shape, size and posture that make up the general 'prey image'. For Wyatt, the goal of good fly design is not exact imitation but the presentation of one or more of these key triggers to elicit the feeding response. This response is not something that fish learn – it is hard-wired into their brains because it makes for efficient feeding.

The rocky pools and tumbling water found in the rivers of western Canada, Scotland and New Zealand call for a highly visible and buoyant fly with instant fish appeal.

A perfect imitation of a natural fly will certainly fool fish, but there is plenty of evidence that many different kinds of animal will respond even more strongly to key triggers when they are presented in an exaggerated – and unrealistic – form. There are also many well known flies that don't look exactly like any particular food item and yet are consistently effective. The Pheasant Tail Nymph and the Gold-Ribbed Hare's Ear clearly possess one or more of these key triggers, and there are plenty of successful flies with over-sized wings, tails, legs or eyes. In behavioural ecology, these exaggerated triggers are known as super-normal stimuli. Wyatt's best-known fly, the Deer Hair Emerger, was a direct product of this line of thinking.

More Is Better

It is thought that when a 'stimulus situation' incorporates several separate and different stimuli, their effects add together to produce an even greater response. This 'Law of Heterogeneous Summation' means it is theoretically possible to create a fly that is more attractive to the fish than the natural is – handy when there's a hatch in progress.

'I throw in with the 'trigger' concept of fly design. I put a lot of stock into the shape and posture of a trout fly, the most important of such triggers…' **Bob Wyatt**

THE DHE

Al Caucci's Comparadun, with its fan-like deer hair wing, was one of several inspirations behind the Deer Hair Emerger.

What, then, are the key triggers that stimulate fish to take emerging nymphs? Bob Wyatt's answer to this is the wing and the sunken abdomen that hangs beneath the surface film. In his quest to endow a durable and easily tied fly with these triggers in a larger-than-life form he turned to the tough and buoyant deer hair wing found on Fran Better's Haystack and Usual and on Al Caucci's Comparadun, and to the submerged abdomen of Hans van Klinken's Klinkhåmer Special.

The resultant fly – the Deer Hair Emerger – floats well but sits low in the water with the abdomen hanging down almost vertically, making it visible to the fish from a distance. Wyatt advises applying floatant to the thorax and the

wing if necessary but not to the abdomen, ensuring that it penetrates the surface. In his words, the fly is tied for vulnerability – it's an easy meal.

In the original version of the fly, the deer hair wing was tied in with the tips pointing forwards and the butt ends were cut off square before the abdomen was dubbed with hare's ear and ribbed with the tag end of the thread, and the relatively short thorax of dubbed hare's ear was then wound from the eye back to the base of the wing, supporting the wing in an upright position. Since then Wyatt has implemented several changes, such as dubbing the abdomen before the wing is tied in and setting the wing further back on the hook shank, leaving more room for a substantial thorax, which Wyatt feels is important to the pattern. The waste ends are now trimmed off at a shallow angle, forming a shoulder that extends part-way down the abdomen.

There are many variations on this basic pattern, for example using mono for the rib, dubbing the thorax with crumpled deer hair for extra buoyancy or giving the fly a CDC wing in place of the deer hair, but in all cases the aim is to create a simple, buoyant fly with a good wing profile and an evident subsurface abdomen.

THE SNOWSHOE HARE EMERGER

Bob Wyatt's own major variation on the DHE uses the soft white hair from the pad of the snowshoe hare in its winter pelt in place of deer hair for the wing. This equally buoyant material is more manageable than deer hair and can therefore be used to tie much smaller flies, down to a #20.

Other Wyatt patterns include the Deer Hair Sedge, the Greyboy Buzzer and the Dirty Duster, as well as a simplifed version of the Hare's Ear Nymph, all formulated on the same principles.

The insulative and water repellent fur of the snowshoe hare's feet, which is as buoyant as deer's hair, much finer and far less fragile, makes ideal material for dry fly wings.

Gooseneck Chironomid

YEAR: 2005   **FLY TYER:** Hermann Fischer   **LOCATION:** British Columbia, Canada

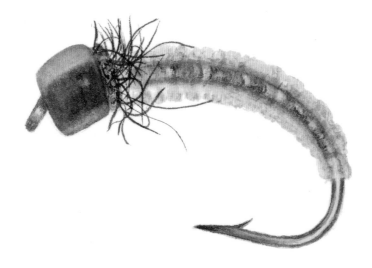

The Original Recipe

Hook
Scud or curved shank nymph, #8–#16

Underbody
Pearlescent tinsel

Thread
Black tying thread

Body
Oil-filled stretch tubing, double wrapped

Head
Two-tone glass bead

Collar
Synthetic black peacock dubbing

The introduction of man-made materials such as closed-cell foam, Mylar, quick-setting resins, synthetic dubbing and holographic fibres in recent decades has opened a world of new possibilities. Among the most versatile of these is stretch tubing, available in a range of diameters and colours under several brand names and capable of imparting a range of lifelike qualities.

SEE-THROUGH SHEEN

Stretch tubing can be used in the tying of a wide variety of flies, but with its shiny surface and translucence it lends itself particularly well to larva, pupa and nymph patterns. In its smallest size it is ideal for tying chironomids, to which it brings an impression of gases within the pupa. Hermann Fischer of Kamloops, British Columbia, has probably done more than any other fly tyer to explore the potential of this material. Informed by his knowledge of the appearance and behaviour of larvae and nymphs, which he has studied in his local lakes and in fish tanks, his creations are supremely realistic. His flies have featured in several books, and in 2003 he was awarded the BC Federation of Flyfishers' Jack Shaw Fly Tying Award.

TYING TECHNIQUES

Fischer is a strong advocate of filling the tubing with mineral oil, not only for colour but more importantly because it renders the tube incompressible so that it retains its cylindrical form, giving the body of the fly a more defined segmentation. When there is only air in the tubing it tends to become flattened when any tension is put on it.

Hermann Fischer strongly recommends double wrapping, starting at the head of the fly and wrapping back to the tail, gradually increasing the tension to give the body a taper. Keeping the tubing under tension, he then uses marker pens to add subtle colour to the tubing before wrapping forward again, easing the tension to exaggerate the taper. This creates a truly three-dimensional look, creating a translucent outer shell through which the digestive tract or other internal parts of the larva are visible. Double wrapping, rather than tying the tubing in along the back or side of the body and then just wrapping forward, also helps to create a balanced fly that will not twist in the water on the retrieve.

Fischer's damselfly nymph, bloodworm and stonefly nymph demonstrate the versatility of oil-filled stretch tubing and the realism that can be achieved.

Bionic Bug

YEAR: 2006   **FLY TYER:** Stu Tripney   **LOCATION:** Otago, New Zealand

The Original Recipe

Hook
2XL wet fly, #6

Thread
Black tying thread

Underbody and Tail
Closed cell foam strip

Head
Foam cylinder with
plastic doll eyes

Body
Metallic dubbing

Back
Closed cell foam strip

Sight post
Fluorescent synthetic yarn

Wing and Hackle
Synthetic hackle fibres

Scottish-born Stuart Tripney moved to New Zealand in the late 1990s, attracted by the exceptional fishing opportunities there, but he soon found that the large browns and rainbows were generally a good deal more wary than those in his home country. A professional fly tyer, guide and fly shop owner, he came up with his own solutions, and in 2006 his Bionic Bug won the gold medal in an international fly tying competition.

FUR, FEATHERS – AND FOAM

Given the pains that generations of fly tyers have gone to to keep their flies on the surface, it is surprising that closed cell foam isn't more widely used, but Stu has done a lot to put that right. Many of his creations look more like cartoon characters than anything a trout might recognise, but the fish find them irresistible nonetheless.

Equally at home on still and moving waters, and great in rough runs and pocket water, foam flies are generally straightforward to tie, and the material is easy to come by, easy to work with and available in every colour under the sun. They can be tied in any size from tiny emergers to large terrestrials that, unlike some larger types of fly, are still light enough to be cast smoothly. These flies can be fished like a standard dry fly on a dead drift or presented more like a popper, with a noisy landing and a ripple-producing strip.

A fly tyer since the age of ten, when he was already using synthetic materials, Stu Tripney offers casting lessons and guided fly fishing trips from his fly shop in Athol, New Zealand.

FOAM FLY FAMILY

The durable and unsinkable Bionic Bug, with its foam strip body and foam cylinder head, offers the trout the silhouette of a drowning terrestrial, while the fluorescent sight post and huge doll's eyes, which Stu feels act as a trigger for the fish, make this fly highly visible to the angler.

His other creations include: the Quiver Bug, which represents a large dragonfly; the iridescent Bionic Beetle that matches summer evening hatches of the metallic green beetle; the small Gnant, a gnat/ant pattern with a white sight post and a parachute hackle tied beneath the hook shank; and the Pogo Nymph, a dubbed Pheasant Tail lookalike with a foam wing case.

Takayama Sakasa Kebari

YEAR: Traditional   **FLY TYER:** Anon.   **LOCATION:** Gifu Prefecture, Japan

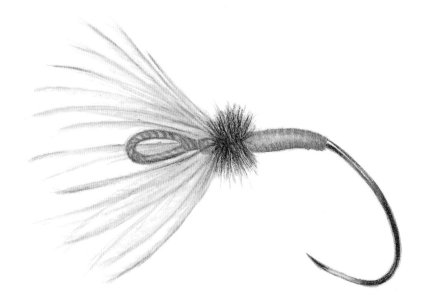

The Original Recipe

Hook
Barbless, eyeless, curved shank, wide gape, #8–#14

Hackle
Soft hackle (e.g. ringneck pheasant, Hungarian partridge)

Thread
Red tying silk

Thorax
Three strands of peacock herl

Eye
Red braid whipped to hook shank

Abdomen
Red tying silk

This fly could equally well have appeared as the first one in this book, as it comes from the Japanese tradition of tenkara fishing that dates back hundreds, if not thousands, of years. Takayama Sakasa Kebari (High-mountains Inverted Feather-needle) is just one of the many flies developed for catching trout in the narrow, tumbling streams of the Japanese highlands using a rod and line method that had almost died out in Japan by the 1980s. This minimalist technique has found a new life among Western anglers in the last decade.

TENKARA

Fly fishers tend to feel more pure than bait chuckers, and dry fly anglers feel superior to the wet fly contingent, but tenkara devotees can look down on us all. This is the ultimate in ultra-lightweight fishing – a long, slender rod, a length of line and a fly. No fly line, no backing, no rod rings, no reel. Dame Juliana would have recognised the outfit immediately, but she would have been very envious of the technology. The traditional bamboo wand has given way to a telescopic graphite rod, typically between 10ft (3m) and 15ft (4.5m) in length, with a fine tip and a piece of braid, called a lillian, at the end. To this is attached a level or tapered leader, a length of tippet and a single fly.

One possible meaning of 'tenkara' is 'from the heavens', and one of the great advantages of this method is that there is no line on the water to spook the fish. The rod is held high so that the rod and line form a 90-degree angle and the fly is delivered directly on to the surface or down to the fish beneath the water. It can then be trotted and manipulated through fish-holding pockets with a natural, drag-free drift on waters that would present a problem to a standard Western fly fishing set-up. When fishing a wet fly, this method has a lot in common with Czech, French and particularly Spanish nymphing, with its long rods and long rigs (see page 174).

The tenkara style of fishing is ideally suited to narrow mountain streams with lots of pocket water and limited space for a back cast.

TENKARA FLIES

Although tenkara flies can be tied on Western-style hooks, the traditional hook is barless and has no eye or spade end. The line attachment is made by whipping a loop of braided silk to the shank before tying the fly.

The Sakasa Kebari is one of the many types of fly used in tenkara fishing, a range that in many respects mirrors some of the more impressionistic Western freshwater nymphs and dry flies. Stewart, Skues and Nemes would have no difficulty understanding the rationale behind many of these patterns and, indeed, starling-hackle spiders are used by tenkara anglers.

Other patterns include long and short soft-hackles, and short stiff hackles, with both 'normal' and reverse hackle styles. The latter tend to be tied with slimmer bodies. In addition, there is a range of Western flies that work well when fished using a tenkara rod, including a small Elk Hair Caddis, Adams dry fly, a tiny Woolly Bugger and many traditional nymphs.

A typical tenkara line is between 10ft and 13ft (3-4m) in length, and horsehair lines are available for the true traditionalist.

REVERSED HACKLE

Sakasa is a style that comprises a soft hackle forming a forward-facing cone over the head, a thorax of peacock herl and a tapering silk thread body. It is tied in a range of colours and, by varying the weight of the hook and the nature of the hackle, can be tied as a wet fly, an emerger or a dry fly. Because the hackle effectively obscures the small thread head, some tyers prefer to tie the fly from front to back with the hook eye in the vice, starting with the head and whip finishing at the bend of the hook.

Leisenring and Hidy would particularly appreciate the reverse hackle. The hackle on a flymph is designed to stand out from the body of the fly and to pulse in the current, so for fast-moving water what could be more logical than tying the hackle so that it faces into the current and cannot be flattened against the hook shank? Part of the tenkara fishing technique is to work the rod tip and impart that pulsing motion to the hackle as the fly moves through the water.

PRESENTATION VS. IMITATION

The Amano Kebari (top) and the Ishigaki Kebari are the only flies tied or fished by Mr Katsutoshi Amano and Dr Hisao Ishigaki respectively.

Like the North Country Spiders, tenkara flies do not represent specific insects, and using imitative patterns is not in the spirit of tenkara fishing. At the heart of the method lie simplicity, minimalism and presentation, the aim being to present the fly to the fish 'where it lives' as accurately as possible. The actual fly is far less important than it is in the Western tradition, and there are purists who claim that one should only ever need one type of fly. That may be a bit extreme, but the Japanese masters of the art do use a very limited number of patterns.

PROS AND CONS

Lightness is tenkara's first great quality, making it ideal for hiking and backpacking, and the rod and line can be set up in moments. The technique is perfect for catching small wild fish on small wild streams where a back cast may not be possible – the kinds of conditions that it was invented for – and here the method provides great drag-free presentation and the possibility of covering water quickly and efficiently.

For larger fish on larger waters it has its limitations. Although the rods are made in greater strengths and greater lengths, the technique requires the rod to be sensitive and to have a fine tip. Since you can't give line to a running fish, tippet strengths have to be kept down if the rod is to survive, and the result can be a lost fish, hook and tippet.

The line is longer than the rod, so the fish has to be brought to hand by holding the leader, providing another opportunity for a large fish to break the line. The tenkara method is also difficult to use in windy conditions, or on very clear waters where spooky fish won't let you get close enough.

CATCHING ON

In the few short years since tenkara first reached North America, the sport has come a long way. Websites and blogs are popping up, English and European anglers are giving it a go and major manufacturers are now producing the super-light telescopic rods. Even some diehard traditional fly anglers are acknowledging that a tenkara rod has its place on the rack.

Western wet and dry flies are being fished on tenkara set-ups and some patterns are being adapted to the tenkara style. Methods, too, are being blended. Wet fly tenkara has a lot in common with American short-line, high-stick nymphing and with Czech, French and Spanish nymphing, and tenkara young bloods in Europe and the USA are already incorporating elements of these other methods, including French indicators and floating bite indicators. No doubt tenkara purists will look down on them, too.

The modern lightweight graphite tenkara rod telescopes down to a handy size for the backpack.

The tip of a tenkara rod has a short length of braid, called a lillian, to which the line is attached.

Bibliography

John Bailey, *Reflections from the Water's Edge*, The Crowood Press Ltd, 1987

Brian Clarke & John Goddard, *The Trout and the Fly*, Lyons Press, 2005

Harry Darbee & Mac Francis, *Catskill Flytier: My Life, Times, and Techniques*, Lippincott, 1977

John Goddard, *Trout Flies of Stillwater*, A & C Black Publishers Ltd, 1979

Terry Hellekson, *Fish Flies – The Encyclopedia of the Fly Tier's Art*, Gibbs Smith, 2005

Andrew Herd, *The History of Fly Fishing*, Medlar Press, 2011

Lefty Kreh, *Saltwater Fly Patterns*, Globe Pequot Press, 1995

Left Kreh, *Lefty Kreh's Ultimate Guide to Fly Fishing*, The Lyons Press, 2003

Terry Lawton, *Marryat: Prince of Fly Fishers*, Medlar Press, 2010

Art Lingren, *Fly Patterns of British Columbia*, Frank Amato Publications Inc., 2008

Chris Mann & Robert Gillespie, *Shrimp and Spey Flies for Salmon and Steelhead*, Stackpole Books, 2001

C. B. McCully, *The Language of Fly-Fishing*, Taylor & Francis, 2000

Steve Raymond, *Blue Upright: The Flies of a Lifetime*, Lyons Press, 2004

John Roberts, *Guide to River Trout Flies*, The Crowood Press Ltd, 1989

Tom Rosenbauer, *The Orvis Fly-Tying Guide*, Globe Pequot Press, 2003

John Shewey, *Spey Flies & Dee Flies: Their History and Construction*, Frank Amato Publications Inc., 2002

Mike Valla, *Tying Catskill-Style Dry Flies*, Headwater Books, 2009

Mike Valla, *The Founding Flies: 43 American Masters, Their Patterns and Influences*, Stackpole Books, 2013

C.F. Walker, *Lake Flies and Their Imitations*, Herbert Jenkins, 1960

For a comprehensive list of books that deal with the history of soft-hackled flies and flymphs, visit www.flymph.com/html/articles.html

An enormous number of older books, including all of the following, can be downloaded free from the internet in pdf form. Some are text only but the majority are high quality colour scans of the originals, and they all make fascinating reading. The principle

sources are the Internet Archive (archive.org), the Gutenberg Project (www.gutenberg.org) and the Biodiversity Heritage Library (www.biodiversitylibrary.org).

Dame Juliana Berners (Barnes), *A Treatyse of Fysshynge wyth an Angle* (1496)

George C. Bainbridge, *The Fly Fisher's Guide* (1816)

Thomas Barker, *The Art of Angling* (1653)

W. Blacker, *Art of Angling* (1842)

Charles Bowlker, *Art of Angling* (1854)

Sydney Buxton, *Fishing and Shooting* (1902)

H. Cholmondeley-Pennell, *The Modern Practical Angler* (1870)

Harfield H. Edmonds and Norman N. Lee, *Brook and River Trouting* (1916)

Richard Franck, *Northern Memoirs* (1658)

Edward Fitzgibbon, *A Handbook of Angling* (1865)

Francis Francis, *A Book on Angling* (1867)

Frederic M. Halford, *Dry-fly Fishing in Theory and Practice* (1889)

Frederic M. Halford, *Floating Flies and How to Dress Them* (1886)

Frederic M. Halford, *The Dry-fly Man's Handbook* (1913)

William Henderson, *Notes and Reminiscences of My Life as as Angler* (1876)

George Parker Holden, *The Idyl of the Split-Bamboo* (1920)

H. G. Hutchinson, *Fly-Fishing in Salt and Fresh Water* (1851)

George M. Kelson, *The Salmon Fly* (1895)

Alexander Mackintosh, *The Driffield Angler* (1821)

Mary Orvis Marbury, *Favorite Flies and Their Histories* (1892)

Leonard Mascall, *A Booke of Fishing with Hooke and Line* (1590)

Martin E. Mosely, *The Dry-fly Fisherman's Entomology* (1921)

Thaddeus Norris, *The American Angler's Book* (1864)

James Ogden, *Ogden on Fly Tying* (1887)

T.E. Pritt, *North-Country Flies* (1886)

G.P.R. Pulman, *The Vade-Mecum of Fly-Fishing for Trout* (1851)

Acknowledgements:

A great many people have helped me in the writing of this book, but I would especially like to thank the following for their advice, comments, contacts, information and photographs: William Anderson, John Bailey, John Barnum, Brian Chan, Roy Christie, Oliver Edwards, Hermann Fischer, Bob Hetzler, Lance Hidy, Hans van Klinken, Lefty Kreh, Holger Lachmann, Bob Popovics, Steve Schalla, Ed Smith, Rob Smith, Jon Ward-Allen, Simon J. Ward and Dave and Emily Whitlock.

I would also like to thank Dee Costello and Lindsey Johns for their patience, professionalism and constant good humour.

William Radcliffe, *Fishing from the Earliest Times* (1921)

Louis Rhead, *American Trout-Stream Insects* (1914)

Alfred Ronalds, *The Fly-Fisher's Entomology* (1883)

William Scrope, *Days and Nights of Salmon Fishing* (1885)

G.E.M. Skues, *Minor Tactics of the Chalk Stream* (1910)

G.E.M. Skues, *The Way of a Trout with a Fly* (1921)

W.C. Stewart, *The Practical Angler* (1867)

Thomas Tod Stoddart, *The Angler's Companion to the Rivers and Lochs of Scotland* (1847)

Michael Theakston, *British Angling Flies* (1862)

Robert Venables, *The Experienced Angler* (1825)

Henry Wade, *Halcyon* (1861)

Izaak Walton and Charles Cotton, *The Compleat Angler* (1653)

Index

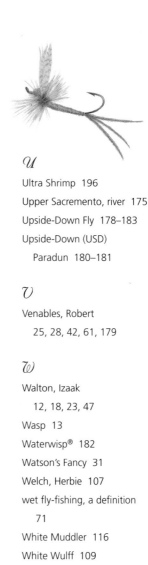

Image credits

Illustrations on cover and pages 10, 16, 22, 30, 32, 38, 44, 46, 52, 56, 60, 66, 72, 76, 84, 88, 94, 98, 102, 106, 108, 112, 114, 118, 122, 128, 130, 133, 136, 140, 144, 150, 154, 158, 162, 164, 167, 170, 172, 176, 178, 184, 188, 194, 198, 200, 206, 210, 212, 214 by Julie Spyropoulos
Illustration on page 190 by Sarah Skeate